A SPECTRUM BOOK

PRENTICE-HALL, INC., Englewood Cliffs, New Jersey 07632

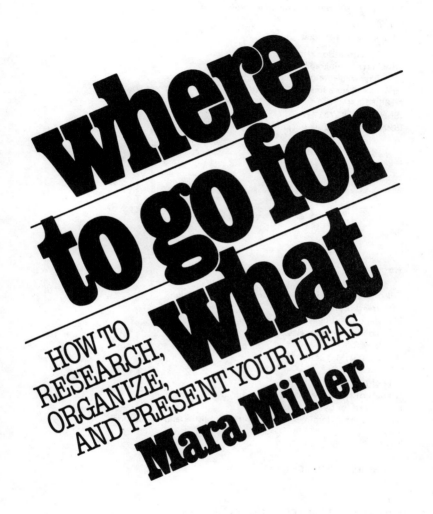

where to go for what

HOW TO RESEARCH, ORGANIZE, AND PRESENT YOUR IDEAS

Mara Miller

M. 649

Library of Congress Cataloging in Publication Data

Miller, Mara.
   Where to go for what.

   (A Spectrum Book)
   Includes bibliographies and index.
   1. Research — Methodology. 2. Information
serivces — User education. I. Title.
Q180.55.M4M54   001.4'2   80-27818
ISBN 0-13-957217-1
ISBN 0-13-957209-0 (pbk.)

001.42
M649w

Editorial production/supervision and interior design
   by *Heath Lynn Silberfeld*
Manufacturing buyer: *Cathie Lenard*
Cover design by *Honi Werner*

A SPECTRUM BOOK

10 9 8 7 6 5 4 3 2

Printed in the United States of America

PRENTICE-HALL INTERNATIONAL, INC., *London*
PRENTICE-HALL OF AUSTRALIA PTY. LIMITED, *Sydney*
PRENTICE-HALL OF CANADA, LTD., *Toronto*
PRENTICE-HALL OF INDIA PRIVATE LIMITED, *New Delhi*
PRENTICE-HALL OF JAPAN, INC., *Tokyo*
PRENTICE-HALL OF SOUTHEAST ASIA PTE. LTD., *Singapore*
WHITEHALL BOOKS LIMITED, *Wellington, New Zealand*

To Jeff

contents

preface

When I finished writing this book, I went back to read it through again. It was then that I realized my chapters titles had somehow changed from what they had been originally. Almost all of them now began with action nouns: "Finding . . ." "Using . . ." "Getting . . ." and so on. It struck me as an odd coincidence.

In retrospect, though, it seems natural that this occurred, for the emphasis of this book is on the *doing* of research — the asking, looking, organizing, imagining, and thinking. As a researcher, I have relied on those methods to find out about subjects. They are what I've described and recommended in these pages.

I should point out that three of the chapters do *not* have active titles. Chapters Six and Seven describe books, magazines, data bases, lists, and other types of information that you should know about. Thousands of researchers before you — nonprofessionals and professionals — have found these to be valuable sources. Why shouldn't you benefit from that knowledge? Yet even in these chapters I indicate how and when you use these works as well as what they are.

Nonetheless, Chapters Six and Seven, plus the Appendix, basically are annotated lists. You might even want to treat them as separate from the main body of the book, referring to them only when you've actually embarked on a particular information search.

The other chapters in this book should be read. This is not a reference book. It is rather a collection of ideas, methods, examples, and even tricks about how to get information — any kind of information about any subject, for any purpose. I hope they add up to an interesting story as well. But at the very least, when you've finished reading, you should feel comfortable tackling almost any research project.

The idea for writing this book originated in a Basic Research Skills course I taught at the Womanschool in New York City. I owe the women in my classes many thanks. They helped me, first, by their candor about the problems they faced in trying to "do research" and, second, by their willingness to learn and play at ways of surmounting those obstacles. Because the students came from a wide range of jobs and backgrounds, I learned as much from them about new sources as they did from me about new methods.

This book and I also owe debts of gratitude to three gifted researchers. Matthew Lesko of Washington Researchers, Terrence Connelly, and Joan Scafarello are kindred souls who, like myself, have no formal training in reference or library science. But they are born researchers, constantly exploring, always ready for the chase, eager to find the perfect route to what they need to know. They enjoy talking about their searches, and so I have benefited enormously from their experiences.

I am grateful as well for the work of two friends: Deborah Brokaw who read and typed my final manuscript; and Liz Levy who read, encouraged, asked, empathized, and performed many other functions that helped usher this work into its present state of being.

The mistakes are mine.

Mara Miller

1

introduction: seeking information

Let me state my bias at the start. It is that research — or information-getting — is not a subject. It is rather a process whose basic components are common sense, some intelligence, imagination, and a few specific habits. Anyone can acquire all these characteristics, excepting intelligence. And this book will show you how. Part of the help will be the names and details of specific sources of information.* A familiarity with reference books, libraries, information retrieval systems, and professional organizations will undoubtedly make your work easier. But to a large extent, this book assumes that *you* are a primary information resource yourself and that how you search yourself and equip yourself will determine your success at finding things out. To that end, you ought to develop certain habits that will put you in shape for getting information. In fact, the habits you acquire will be more valuable than any knowledge you are able to memorize about external information sources.

A good professional researcher will tell you that it's better to have an idea about where to go for a fact than to know the fact itself. The good researcher knows it is the process of getting information that's important. Even in those chapters in which I detail specific information centers, such as libraries or associations. I emphasize knowing *how* to approach them and their components — persons, reference works, or data.

Thinking imaginatively about where to go for information and then trying out the various routes imagined are not really special abilities or talents. They are habits. "I couldn't think of the right place to go" is an excuse for an unwillingness to play at getting information. That, in turn, may come from

*The first time a particular reference source is mentioned in these pages a complete citation for it is provided — author or editor, full title, publisher, and dates of publication. From then on, the work is referred to by its title only. All titles, however, appear in the index.

the fear of making a mistake. Practice getting rid of that fear. Indeed, this book rests on a conviction that *any* idea about where to go for information is worth trying — unless, of course, you can think of a better one.

Sometimes knowing the so-called right source can actually hinder an information search. Put another way, a little knowledge can be worse than mere common sense. This latter quality is essential to doing research, particularly for the nonprofessional. Yet many of us have misplaced common sense as we cope with an increasingly specialized and compartmentalized world of information.

If, for example, you were trying to locate the text of a speech made by Senator Gary Hart (Democrat, Colorado) on nuclear energy, and you knew he gave the speech on the Senate Floor sometime this year, how would you obtain a copy? The common sense way is to call or write Senator Hart's office and ask for one. But more than a few who were assigned this question in a research course suggested going through back, unindexed issues of the *Congressional Record* (which does indeed print the full texts of senators' speeches made in Congress). In this instance, knowing about the *Congressional Record* as a source makes the search a more difficult one. This book will often note when it is better *not* to go to a book or library for information. In fact, one chapter will deal exclusively with use of the telephone as a more effective way of getting information. Particularly in your nonwork life, the types of information you seek are more likely to be acquired by means of the telephone. The nonprofessional usually underutilizes this tool. Common sense, again, should dictate to you when it is the better way of finding things out.

THREE BASIC RULES
FOR GETTING INFORMATION

The search for information begins with an idea. Sometimes it's your own idea — you want to find out about a subject; or you need to find out because you want to go somewhere, do something, buy something, try something. Often the idea originates with someone else — your boss, teacher, friend or colleague — but you are asked to get the information. A search is always more difficult if it's not your own idea that begins it. You are not in on the reason for which the information is being sought; *yet you need to know the reason in order to get the best information.* That is the first rule for getting information. Even in cases of what appear to be simple fact-finding requests, you need to know at least a part of the "why" (why is this information being sought?). If the person asking you to get information doesn't fill you in on the reasons (he or she may not know them either), it's up to you to ask before beginning your search. How you find the information, how you understand the search and, in many cases, how you present the found information will depend on the purpose for which it's sought.

Suppose you are asked to find out when penicillin was first used. It seems a straightforward enough request: Just come up with a date. But you still ought to find out why the asker wants to know, because you can come up with the fact that penicillin was first used in 1941, only to then be asked, "Was that in the United States?" "Was that use on humans or on animals only?" and other more specifically phrased parts of the question that were omitted in the first asking. You must be the one to ask for more information about the nature of the search. It would be ideal if you could know the larger idea or concept behind the research being sought, but that's unlikely to happen in most job situations. Just make sure you've obtained some background on the *why* before you start.

A second rule for getting information is: *Always assume that the perfect answer exists.* Whether you're looking for facts, ideas, objects, or services, you have to believe that the answer is out there. First of all, it almost always is; and, second, you'll never go after it with the right degree of zeal and innovation if you suspect for a moment that it doesn't exist. Once you know it's out there, you have only to figure out how to get to it. This rule becomes especially relevant when using libraries and librarians to get information. You will see later in this book how the specificity with which you approach a librarian in seeking information will greatly determine the success of your search. In order to ask questions that are specific, you must have in your mind the idea that the answer exists and that it is so specific it can be described by you. One can better illustrate this rule by borrowing a lesson from another part of the research profession: Picture researchers must deal with thousands of possible "answers." There is no way for a picture researcher to actually know that a particular picture exists (say, an old photograph of the first tennis court in America) unless he or she has seen it before. And that's hardly likely to be the case. But the good picture researcher has an idea (What would be the absolutely perfect illustration for this page in the book?) and then imagines that the answer is out there. It's the only way to find the best answer, although he or she may have to settle for a less-than-perfect one. You, too, may find that after your search, the perfect information you wanted does not exist, or is unobtainable. But you have found out, not merely assumed it, and the difference makes for a greater chance of success in your search.

The only other rule for getting information is this: *Risk making a fool of yourself and risk being wrong.* If you can't face either possibility, you'll never be good at finding out. The nonprofessional's reticence at using the telephone to locate information (willing instead to spend endless hours in a library) in some ways stems from a fear of sounding stupid or foolish. You can learn techniques and routes to follow that will make telephoning easier, or interviewing more effective, but no one can teach you to take risks with your self-esteem. If you want to know something badly enough and want to find it out the quickest way possible, you'll just have to take a deep breath and ask. After a while, you'll realize that you never sound as ignorant to someone else as you do to yourself. And so what if you do? People who have the information you seek are more likely to share it with the hesitant, imperfect asker than they are with either the know-it-all or, certainly, the one who never asked.

It is often repeated in books on research that rule number one is to be accurate. As I can't imagine your wanting bad information, let's assume at the outset that the search for the *best* answer automatically precludes your settling for an easy but invalid one. When you have to prepare original research in the form of a report or paper, you will go through steps of verification and testing of your hypotheses, if only to lend more weight to your claims. But for most of your information purposes, I wouldn't worry about whether you have a proper regard for facts or truths. Drumming in a notion of the "virtues" of a researcher only tends to isolate the searching process further from the grasp of ordinary mortals. I'd rather have you think anyone can do research (almost anyone can) than that you must be a rather special person in order to even attempt this game.

And that brings me to the final thesis of this book, which is that getting information is fun. It is in many ways like a game (admitting that the purposes and methods are often quite serious). I think it no mere coincidence that research has been described by those who do it as "detection," "the hunt," "hide and seek," and a number of other sportlike activities. If you will think of getting information as a process that is really just an extension of "Twenty Questions," "Botticelli," or even "Who made the only unassisted triple play in a baseball game?" you'll be better able to understand searching and how to play at it. You will also be inching closer to the fun of finding out and the search's ultimate reward: being able to say, with certainty, "I've got it!"

2

using yourself as a resource

Whether the kind of research you want to do involves finding out isolated facts, developing a lengthy project, or locating a particular person, place, object, or service, the first assessment you must make is of yourself. You are your own best resource when it comes to getting information.

KNOWING WHAT YOU ALREADY KNOW

For one thing, you know your own history, and as you will soon discover, your past and present are valuable aids in getting information.

A researcher must ask, then answer, two questions: "What is it I need to know?" and "What is it I already know?" The second question stops most nonprofessionals cold. "I haven't been in the reference room of a library since school days," is a remark often made by working men and women. "I don't remember anything." Yet you do know quite a lot of information already; the trick is to learn how to apply and associate what you *do* know with what you do not know and want to find out.

Some people associate naturally: You say "America's Cup" for instance, and they say, "Oh, yes, I always notice the cover of a magazine called *Yachting* when I buy my paper each morning," or "I was in Newport once; don't they race out of there?" The person who answers thus doesn't yet have any hard facts about the America's Cup but already has a head start on how and where to get the information (call the magazine, or check its index for articles about the races; call or write the Newport Visitors' Bureau; find out if there's a committee up there that sponsors or puts out information about the races).

The calls may or may not produce facts, but they will at least lead to other sources — books, magazines, experts — that *will* result in hard information about the races.

Most of us, however, are not free associaters and need practice in making these connections.

Suppose you want to find out the following: the name of a Hitchcock movie starring Cary Grant and Joan Fontaine in which she marries him, then begins to suspect that he is trying to murder her. Let's require, though, that you must find out the name of this movie only by asking someone you know personally. First, imagine the perfect source for this information. Whom do you know who comes closest to being that source? Unless you know the answer yourself or are a friend of Hitchcock, Grant, or Fontaine, you're going to have to think of a friend or acquaintance whose job or, more likely, whose outside interests makes him or her the right resource. Describe the person you know whom you'll ask. What made you choose him or her? If you think about it for a moment you can probably come up with the name of someone who is, say, a Hitchcock buff and knows the plots of all his movies; or someone who is a Cary Grant fan and has seen most of his films; or someone who merely likes movies in general and collects books about them. There's always the possibility that you know someone whose profession makes him the perfect source — in this case a film reviewer or archivist would be ideal — but in most instances you'll call a person whose hobby or interest *you know about and associate with* what you want to find out. And that's the point: You know or have met probably one hundred people who have special interests (and thus perhaps books and collections on these interests) that you can, if you think about it, recall.

If you don't believe this, and even if you do, this exercise should prove helpful: Make a list of twenty persons you know. Start with your closest friends and family, then job colleagues, then people you've met but don't know well. For each person named, write down your brief description of what they do for a living and then, under a separate heading, list whatever you know about their outside interests. Does one person collect stamps, drink and know about wine, ski, go to hockey games, or use a camera? In those cases where you know someone's history (close friends and family), make a separate third heading for that: Where are they from? Where have they traveled? What other jobs have they had? After one or two of these, you should realize that almost everyone you know, although not an expert, has knowledge about areas with which you are unfamiliar. You needn't file this information on cards — though I know at least one person who does — but you ought to remember that your friends and acquaintances are information resources for you, just as you in some way serve as a resource for them when they seek certain facts or "leads."

You know more than just your intimate circle, though. Suppose you now want to find out the answer to that same question, but this time with the stipulation that you call only someone you do *not* know. Whom will you try and why? Here, you might call the film reviewer on your local paper or television station; or you might know to call the reference librarian at your library (more on this resource in Chapter Five); but there are a myriad of other possibilities. Film rental companies, a local movie house that specializes in showing old films, a college film department, Cary Grant's agent, Hitchcock's studio, a cinema bookstore — these are a few leads you might try. Some of these are apt to have the information at their fingertips. Others will lead to another, better source. And some are far-fetched and may net nothing. But the point of the exercise is to make you begin a line of "connections." You ought to realize that even though you don't know the absolutely right film library, archive, or book to go to for this information, you do know several ways of finding out — any of which can lead you to the best source. You simply have to think about the search from the point of view of what you do already know.

It's useful to do a few exercises like the above to get yourself in the habit of associating information you don't know with that which you do.

Try a few of the following (again with the two separate requirements: one source you know personally and one you don't): How would you get in touch with the scientist Linus Pauling? Who holds the record for the most stolen bases in a single season? What are the lyrics to "This Could Be the Start of Something Big?" Again, for each, try to imagine that the perfect source does exist. What would it be and how would you get to it? In the case of finding a person, ask yourself, Does anyone you know know him or her? Is anyone you know likely to know *about* that person, be able to fill you in on the kinds of details that make a person-search easier. In the case of Linus Pauling, it might help you to know that he wrote a book about Vitamin C and the common cold. Who published it? Can you get to him through the publisher? Or, if you know that he is a professor at X University, you can try tracking him through there. Or, if someone you know knows that Pauling has spoken at a college or group meeting, you can go through that institution to find the name of his agent or speakers' bureau. Each of these steps may be pursued by telephone and even the $2 telephone call to Stanford University in California (which is where Pauling taught) may cost you less than a trip to the library.

An additional benefit of these exercises is that they get you to use the telephone. Most men and women who do not do research for a living feel uncomfortable in library reference rooms and thus deduce that they cannot get information the best way possible. But in many cases the best way is the telephone, and exercises that get you on the telephone asking for facts start you on your way to being a successful searcher. (See Chapter Four for a closer examination of the telephone as an information tool and how to use it.)

Let's return to a consideration of yourself as a resource. Who are you and what do you already know is the way we're now phrasing the question. If you feel uncomfortable citing yourself as an authority on any subject, search yourself in the same way you just investigated your friends' research potential.

Fill out this form: First, state your job or occupation if you have one, then a one-sentence description of what you do at work. "House manager" is an occupation, too, so say so if you are one. If you went to college, list your major and minor; if you've taken any course since high school, write that down as well. Next, list five books you've read in the past year that were not required by your job (they may have been chosen for self-improvement purposes, they may be serious or light fiction or nonfiction). Then list any newspapers to which you subscribe or buy more than twice a week. List any magazines or other periodicals to which you subscribe, noting whether you receive them as part of your job or not. List those magazines you buy only occasionally at newsstands. Now list those subjects about which you think you have some knowledge, either because of your job, schooling, or outside interests. You're obviously not a professional expert, but use a broad brush here. Include anything you know, whether it's Mexican restaurants, Fellini movies, metaphysics, or children's toys. List any associations or clubs to which you belong, professional and/or social. List the last five places you've visited outside your home state. List the last five exhibits you've seen (museums, libraries, corporate displays, sidewalk shows, or others). Do you collect anything? Write it down — anything at all, playbills, seashells, whatever it is. Last, do you have a filing system (folders, cards, boxes, baskets) at work, at home or both? List the category headings you use in your files, even if you never actually write down specific subject headings on your file folders. (I know one woman who keeps a large grocer's carton filled with clippings, articles, and notes she's kept that have anything to do with women writers. She's never actually written down that heading, "Women Writing," but she knows what sort of things are in the box, and that's the closest she could come to describing its contents.) Include any boxes you have lying around, too, on your lists, as well as recipe files, maps, catalogs, and the like. You must realize that if you read, clip, or collect something, it is a resource that you can tap sometime in the future. If you go so far as to file what you clip under actual subject headings, you're already the kind of person who thinks about the likelihood of needing information and doing future research.

If you accept now that you are a research resource because of what you see and do, whom you know, and what you keep, it shouldn't prick your confidence greatly to recognize that you're probably not as good a resource as you ought to be. Presumably, you're reading this book to become a better one. And there are ways to do it that have nothing to do with libraries, data banks, and footnotes.

First of all, you must become a reader. To get information, you have to be a reader, and by that I mean you must acquire the *habit* of reading. It is not essential that you read entire books, or even parts of books, to start, but you must begin to use your eyes to read things: advertisements, book spines, newspaper headlines, articles, brochures, books. Beware of television. Television may indeed impart information, but I think your relationship to that medium is always as a "watcher;" a watcher is not only *not* a reader but unlikely to become one. If you do watch television regularly, I can only advise you to make it the very last thing you do in the day. It's a habit that competes successfully with the habit of using your eyes to read.

Read a newspaper. Very few people read entire newspapers, and it's not even a good idea, but skim the paper, reading at least one complete article in it. Reading a paper is not just important for the information you'll obtain (some argue that there's very little hard information in newspapers these days), but again for its value as a habit. You'll begin to get an idea of how a newspaper is laid out. Read a newsweekly magazine — again, not cover to cover, but through it. You'll find later that when you need a starting point in finding out *about* a subject, back issues of the newsweeklies — *Time* and *Newsweek* — are going to be your best bets. You'll be way ahead if by that time you're familiar with their layouts, subject headings, and regular features.

Make yourself read one general piece of information daily (that is, something not related to your job). It will get your eyes in shape; it will start your associative powers moving too. Pretty soon you will have acquired the habit of making connections between something you've "seen" and information you need to know. There is one printed piece of information I'd recommend above all others to get you in the habit of thinking as an information gatherer — the Sunday Book Review section of the *New York Times*. One week's collection of articles, reviews, interviews, and lists therein is the quickest way I know to have a sense of the kinds of information that exist *out there.* Most of the information will stay with you, too. And you will be surprised at how one day when you need to, you will recall that there *is* a book on the subject of mushrooms, or another on the petroleum industry. This is a more important research asset than having actually read the book, and it's a facility that will serve you well.

Another important means by which you'll acquire the habit of reading and knowing where information lies is by hanging out in bookstores. Hanging out in a library is difficult: You're not likely to go there without a specific purpose in mind, and the information in libraries is too plentiful and too spread out for a quick-read. There is also less visual stimuli in libraries (except in "new books" sections, which may account for everyone's stopping there no matter what their purpose in going to the library). Part of the habit we're aiming to acquire is the use of your eyes for the quick-read, and bookstores are better suited to this purpose. They're colorful, attractive places, but in a lower key than most stores. One can say "I'm just looking" in a bookstore with less self-consciousness than one can in another kind of store or even a library. Bookstores contain a lot of information (again, not necessarily *in* the books, but the books themselves). Browse through the sections of a bookstore on a regular basis and you'll be surprised how much you retain of the information that is out there and available to you.

If you've acquired a regular habit of quick-reading, you're ready to file. Filing *as a habit* is almost as essential to information-getting as is reading. You must maintain files of some kind and, if you do already, you must make them better. I don't care what kinds of material you choose to keep; what's important is that you clip, organize, and keep, by categories, some information because you want to have it. You can use folders, shoe boxes, card files, whatever you like. Some people use all three. But you must begin breaking down information that is important to you into orderly categories.

Several of your categories may be large catchalls: "Things that Strike My Fancy," "Ideas I Have," "In the Works;" others may be quite specific — stores and services, jobs, organizations. The point is that you learn to rely on your files, which means developing a filing system you can call on to provide you (or others) with useful information. Determining how precise or vague your subject headings will be should be based on frequency of use and usefulness to you. If "Ideas I Have" works for you and you know exactly what's in there and how to find it, that's fine. You need no further subdivision. But if there's an error in your files it's most likely on the side of too vague a heading and too large a folder.

Start with the basics: Everyone has files of one sort or another covering personal finances — taxes, checks, receipts, bills — pieces of paper and forms you have to keep, perhaps for several years. If yours are labelled merely "money" or "finances," they can't be serving you well. When you go to them for information I'll bet it takes a while to find the specific item you need. Start all over again and reorganize what you keep into smaller folders (or boxes, or drawers if that's what you use). "Receipts" should be separated from "investments," and depending on the extent of what you spend or invest, each of those might be subdivided further — investments into "stocks and bonds," "insurance," and "banks" for instance.

If you are the person in your home who is responsible for its maintenance and operation, one of your folders absolutely must be "warranties and instructions" (maybe adding "catalogs" here as well), unless you've unplugged yourself successfully from electronic life. The files of the house-manager should contain also a "stores and services" section, in which you keep business cards, advertisements, bills, and notes on specific jobs or stores (or how will you know, when you go to have your house repainted, what they charged you last time, which company did the better job, etc.). One other subject heading to have is "correspondence (business)" for each year, into which you place copies of any and all letters written or received that relate to services, contracts, fines — communications that are nonjob and nonpersonal.

Other categories in your filing system will depend on what you do. If you're a writer, for instance, a category "Ideas I Have" is too broad and should be broken down, perhaps into "Proposals," "In the Works," "First Drafts," and then some more, by subjects or the specific ideas themselves. If you cook a lot, your recipes or food files will no doubt be subdivided into "sauces," "salads" and other categories much smaller than these. No matter what profession or field you're in, your files at home ought to reflect the several aspects of your life: job, home, hobbies, ideas, and even fantasies. For if these were not important to you, why would you notice certain items, read them, tear them out, and keep them?

One note of warning about files. They should be made up of those items you see and for one reason or another want to save. Don't go looking for items to stick in your files, unless you're about to begin a major research project. You will soon run out of storage space if you do, and the mere thought of opening one of your bulging folders will fill you with dread. In other words, don't let your filing system dictate what you clip, but let what you wish to keep determine the organization of your files.

You may find that a mixture of filing methods works best for you: perhaps a rolodex or card box of names and numbers of people and places you deal with regularly; then financial information in separate folders but kept apart from your other files; then your main files kept on a bookshelf, in a file cabinet, in baskets, or someplace else.

There is no rule that says your files must follow a logical outline. Remember, they are not being kept in preparation for a term paper. They exist to help you work and live, enabling you to lay your hands on the information you're likely to need. If you think the things you'd like to keep seem too frivolous or illogically ordered to organize, consider the following selections from the real-life files of three working people:

1. Oil; Coal; Nuclear Energy; Jogging; Bills; Eugene O'Neill.
2. Apartment Repair-Decor; Subscriptions; Education; Diet and Health.
3. Taxes; Bonds; Stamps; Car; Organizations; Travel; In the Works.

You'll soon be able to tell whether your files are working properly for you. If you dread going near them, because they're loaded with pieces of paper and you don't know which to keep and which to part with, either your subject headings are too broad or you haven't selected the parts of the subjects that really interest you. Go through your largest file folders at least every six months and throw out some of what's there if you haven't referred to it once and/or it no longer seems so interesting.

With an awareness of what you know, what you keep, and, now, how to organize it into useful files, you are almost a complete information resource. But you're not quite ready to move out into the unfamiliar zones of libraries, archives, and experts. Why should you have to if there are questions you can answer and information you can get without leaving your home or office? Whatever kinds of information needs you are apt to have, there are a few specific books, materials, and telephone numbers you ought not to be without.

First and foremost is the telephone directory for your city and its companion volume, the classified or yellow pages directory. Telephone books are the most used and most helpful research tools in existence. When Bob Woodward and Carl Bernstein, the *Washington Post* reporters who pieced together Watergate connections, were trying to track down a signature on a Nixon campaign check belonging to one Kenneth

H. Dahlberg, they relied on the telephone directory. The Florida bank on which the check was drawn knew nothing about Dahlberg or his whereabouts. Woodward asked the *Post* librarian to go through the clipping files for anything on Dahlberg. Back came a photograph showing Senator Hubert Humphrey standing next to a man identified in the caption as Mr. Dahlberg. There was no further information indicating who Dahlberg was, whether he was a Democrat, or where the picture was taken. Reporter Woodward went to the Minneapolis telephone directory (because Minneapolis was the largest city in Humphrey's home state) and there found a listing for a Kenneth H. Dahlberg. He dialed it and reached the right man, who, taken by surprise, admitted his connection to the Nixon Re-election Committee.

In another feat of solid investigative reporting, Selwyn Raab, at the time working for the *World-Telegram and Sun,* was responsible for the acquittal of an innocent George Whitmore on, first, a murder, then a subsequent rape and assault charge in New York City. Whitmore had been held in police headquarters in Brooklyn overnight where, after lengthy interrogation and strongarm techniques, he "confessed" to these crimes among others. Reporter Raab spent over six years finding the information that would establish Whitmore's innocence. In the end, the final rape conviction came down to locating one possible witness whose name appeared in a patrolman's book on that night, six years previous. The witness was named Mrs. Viroet, sister-in-law of the rape victim. She had given the patrolman a description of the assailant that varied greatly from her sister-in-law's testimony. Raab had to find Mrs. Viroet, but all he knew was her name and the fact that she had run a grocery store. So he, Whitmore's lawyer, and a hired private investigator divvied up the New York City telephone books, looking for any "Viroet." Raab recalled:

> I took Manhattan and Brooklyn, and the private investigator started with Queens and the Bronx. And he hit somebody! A Viroet in the Bronx who

said he remembered somebody living in that neigh-
borhood who had moved to Puerto Rico. . . . And
they had run a grocery store . . .[1]

Raab tracked down Mrs. Viroet in Puerto Rico, where she
signed an affadavit to the fact that the man she had seen that
night could not have been George Whitmore. And seven years
after his arrest, Whitmore was acquitted of this final charge.

These examples show how the telephone book can
be used creatively to get information, when all else fails. It is no
less an important tool to someone outside the investigative
occupations. You will discover its usefulness by first exploring
its contents. Get in the habit of using the book to look up
persons' numbers instead of dialing "Information." Take a
look at the section in the telephone book under the heading
"United States Government," which will tell you how many
different agencies have representatives or offices in your town.
Did you know, for example, that if you want a publication put
out by the federal government, you may not have to write to
Washington to get it (which takes about six weeks to fill your
order)? Under "United States Government, Government Printing Office," in your book, you can find out if your city has one
of the 24 federal bookstores in the country; if it does, you can
pick up many government publications there. If you live in a
moderate- to large-size city, the section "United States Government" will be headed by a box of frequently called numbers,
a valuable source of information on matters ranging from seeking a federal job, finding out visiting hours for national parks,
locating a zip code, or requesting secret service protection.

Similarly, if you live in a medium-sized town, there
will be headings in the telephone book under your state's government. Look under "____ (your state), State Government."
Your town or city's government divisions are also listed in the

---

[1] Excerpt from *By-Lines: Profiles in Investigative Journalism* by Elizabeth Levy.
Copyright ©1975 by Elizabeth Levy. Published by Four Winds Press, a Division of
Scholastic Magazines, Inc.

white pages, and a quick one-time look at all of these will give you an idea of resources available to you when the need arises.

Also, when no other leads come to mind, the white pages of the telephone book can start you off on a search for information about a subject. Corporations, associations, and other institutions very often have, as a part of their names, the subject you wish to find out about. A glance in the Manhattan telephone book, for instance, under the word "Ski" nets sixteen entries, of which two are magazines, two are nationwide associations, one a local club, and the rest private companies, stores, or travel agencies. Calling any of the first five of these is bound to lead you to the information you were after on skiing; and you haven't had to leave your desk. In another search, say, for the Hitchock movie we were looking for earlier, the Manhattan directory would give you an endless stream of possibilities under the heading "film." You will find libraries, magazines, clubs, rental companies, all with that word in their titles. If you had not been able to find the information any other way — through a friend or source you knew about — and you had no yellow pages, the white pages would have gotten you started.

It should be apparent by now that you need a copy of the Manhattan telephone directory, whether or not you live there. Add Washington, D.C., too. New York and Washington are the two largest information centers in our country. You can't afford to be without their directories (you needn't telephone either; part of the directory's usefulness is that it gives addresses as well). Your telephone company's business office can get you copies of each. Your library will probably have the directories for other major U.S. cities, but these two are so valuable, you should have them on your bookshelf.

Yellow pages or "classified" directories are sometimes easier reference tools to use because entries are listed by subject, whether or not the subject is part of the company's name. But they are limited by the fact that only some institutions are listed (libraries, schools and clubs) and these are listed not by subject but rather under the general categories of "clubs," "libraries," etc. Occasionally you will find valuable cross-references. Under "Clubs" for instance, it says "see also "Associations," "Fraternal Organizations," and so on. By no means do the listings cover all groups or companies in your town (one must pay to be listed in the yellow pages). Still, when it comes to locating specific products or services, the classified directory will serve.

You must have a dictionary, and unless you're a "word person" who wants to know the most precise definition plus the entire history of each word's usage, you will do fine with an abridged or "college" dictionary. A particularly good volume is *The American Heritage Dictionary of the English Language,* New College Edition (New York: American Heritage, 1975), which also comes in a paperback edition. It is a modern work but still manages to adhere to rules of good, basic English. It provides some etymology (historical background of the word) and a few bonuses such as a complete list of proofreaders' marks, under the entry "proofreaders' marks." Unlike many other dictionaries, *American Heritage* lists proper names within the main body of entries, thus enabling the user to identify quickly a person, place, or common institution. The dictionary, even in its paperback version, has a great many illustrations and photographs. Other suitable desk dictionaries include: *Webster's New World Dictionary of the American Language,* Second College Edition (New York: Simon & Schuster, 1980) and *The Random House College Dictionary,* Revised Edition (New York: Random House, 1975) (which has many illustrations and strives for modern American English). Each of these sells for about $10.

If you want to have at your fingertips every word in the English language and its history of usage, the only dictionary that will do is *The Compact Edition of the Oxford English Dictionary,* James Murray et al., ed., (New York: Oxford University Press, 1971), which comes in two volumes with its own magnifying glass (the print size is tiny as the twelve standard-type volumes of the regular *Oxford English Dictionary* have been reduced into these two volumes without sacrificing a word), and sells for about $95. Supplements to the *Oxford English Dictionary,* which follow English usage up through the twentieth century and recent years, come out as they are compiled. Supplement Volume I, A–G, was published in 1972; Volume II, H–N, in 1976; and Volume III, Q–Z, is expected any year now. The OED is the first-rate authority on our language and its usage. If you wish to do a thorough job of comparing what is available in dictionaries, consult the new and easy-to-read *Dictionary Buying Guide* (New York: Bowker, 1977) by Kenneth Kister, which is in the reference room of your public library.

You need an atlas. The best by far is the *Times Atlas of the World,* Comprehensive ed., 5th ed. (London: Times Books, 1975); but it's oversized (you won't want to use it very often) and costs about $75. Look for smaller ones, such as the paperback *The Penguin World Atlas* (Middlesex, England: Penguin Books, Ltd., 1974). Insurance agents often give out free U.S. Road atlases, which are good resource books, too, but you need a world atlas as well. Some of the large-sized but affordable ($18 to $30 in range) ones are: *The International Atlas,* rev. ed. (Chicago: Rand McNally, 1975); *Medallion World Atlas* (Maplewood, N.J.: Hammond, 1977); and the *Cosmopolitan World Atlas* (Chicago: Rand McNally, 1978). You may want to check *International Maps and Atlases in Print,* K. L. Winch, ed. (New York: Bowker, 1974) for further information.

Figure 2-1. From *The Compact Edition of the Oxford English Dictionary.* Reprinted with permission of Oxford University Press. Copyright © 1971 by Oxford University Press.

Years ago families who could afford to invested in one of the multivolume encyclopedia sets as a matter of course. The most prestigious to own — some say the best — was the *Encyclopaedia Britannica.* It may still be the biggie of the encyclopedia business, but you don't really need it. In fact, I would not recommend an encyclopedia for your personal bookshelf at all except that there are now several affordable, tabletop-size excellent ones, so you needn't repair to the library when you need general information on a subject. The best of these is the *New Columbia Encyclopedia,* 4th ed. (New York: Columbia University Press, 1975), which sells for about $45; it is an excellent biographical reference source as well as a general encyclopedia and provides useful bibliographies for many entries.

If you're going to consider buying a multivolume set, visit the reference room of your library and compare the various editions that are available. You'll want to check each for content, type-size, illustrations, and even weight of the page (*Britannica,* with its tissue-thin pages will either please you — it's supposed to mean you're getting more information in each volume — or drive you crazy). Choose a topic that is modern in scope and allows for illustration — "Advertising" is one; then compare the treatment of this subject in each encyclopedia. The major competitors are: *The New Encyclopaedia Britannica* (Chicago: Encyclopaedia Britannica, 1976); 30 volumes, 15th ed.; *Encyclopedia Americana,* International Edition (New York: Americana Corp., 1976); 30 volumes; and the *World Book Encyclopedia,* 22 volumes (Chicago: Field Enterprises, 1976), ostensibly for young people but a most useful tool for adult researchers, as you shall see. These sets vary enormously from one another. Some have articles signed by scholars; others are anonymously written. Some contain lengthy bibliographies at the end of an entry; others refer the reader to "further reading" within the main body of the entry. These sets cost hundreds of dollars, so explore each thoroughly in the reference room before buying. None of them is essential to your information-getting bookshelf. Consult Kenneth Kister, ed.,

Encyclopedia Buying Guide (N.Y.: Bowker, 1978) before taking an expensive plunge.

You must find out what is available at a large library near where you live or work. Almost every library of a significant size has a piece of printed material explaining its collections and services. These booklets (or sometimes just a single sheet of information) will save you time, even if your contact with the library will be primarily by telephone. Obtain a copy from your library and keep it on your bookshelf. Larger libraries with major research divisions may offer more detailed pamphlets explaining how to use their collections. Even if you do not live near one of the larger library systems, you ought to know how a major library operates. Your own library will be a scaled-down version of that. Write to one or two of the libraries listed below and ask for their guides or bulletins.

Major U.S. Public Libraries
_____

| New York | New York Public Library, Main Branch, 42nd Street and Fifth Avenue, New York, New York 10036. (1) *It's Your Library: A Guide to Publicly Supported Libraries in the Bronx, Manhattan and Staten Island* (with map and key telephone numbers, it is free); (2) *To the Undergraduate* (a simply written folder "designed to tell you which part of the NYPL will best serve your needs," free); and (3) *Guide to the Research Libraries of the New York Public Library* (which details all collections and services; it is sometimes free but at other times costs 25¢). |

Chicago	Chicago Public Library, 425 North Michigan Avenue, Chicago, Illinois 60611; Central Reference and Research Library (same address); Chief of General Information Services Division.
Los Angeles	Los Angeles Public Library, 630 West Fifth Street, Los Angeles, California 90017. *Operation Los Angeles Public Library.*
Boston	Boston Public Library, 666 Boylston Street, Box 286, Boston, Massachusetts 02117. Reader Services.
Houston	Houston Public Library, Civic Center, 500 McKinney Avenue, Houston, Texas 77002. Public Information Office.

Another library whose services you must know about is our national library, The Library of Congress. Its 18 million books and 58 million other treasures (microfilms, files, etc.) are available to the public under certain circumstances and conditions. The Library of Congress also provides special research services, sometimes charging an hourly fee for a major project search. Write for their two booklets — *Services to the Nation* and *Information to Readers* — at The Library of Congress, Washington, D.C. 20540. (See Chapter Five for more information about Library of Congress services and collections.)

In looking for information about a library near where you live, bear in mind that universities, colleges, and sometimes corporations also print guides to their facilities. If your nearest library does not have such material, consult the *American Library Directory*, edited by Jaques Cattell Press, (New York: Bowker, 1923 to date), a copy of which it will have. In this directory, which is issued every two years, you can look up your state, then your town or one nearby. The entry will tell you, for each library, the nature of the facility — public, college, corporate, club, etc. — the extent of its collection, special interests, names of librarians, telephone numbers, procedures for use, and many other details.

At least half the information one wants to know in an average lifetime can be found in the government. Economic statistics, census data, questions of law, contents of bills or speeches, the availability of funds for specific local programs — these are merely a few of the information needs with which citizens turn to government. The dilemma is knowing which agency or bureau to call or write with which kind of request. The answer lies in government manuals or yearbooks, usually published on an annual basis, by your state, local, and federal governments. You should obtain copies of each, though they need not be the most recent editions. What you're after is an

Figure 2-2. From the *American Library Directory,* 32nd Edition. Reprinted with permission of R. R. Bowker Company. Copyright © 1979 by Xerox Corporation.

S   NINETY-NINES, INC LIBRARY, 5435 E Young Rd, (Mail add: PO Box 59965, Will Rogers World Airport, Oklahoma City, 73159). Tel 812-337-1798, 332-4065; & 405-685-7969. *Librn* Dorothy R Niekamp. Staff 3 (prof 1, nonprof 2)
Founded 1974
Ann Exp Bks $500
Library Holdings: Bk titles 150; Per sub 1, vols bd 45; AV — Flm, Maps
Subject Interests: Basic aviation & women in aviation

BLUFFTON — 8297. Area code 219

P   BLUFFTON-WELLS COUNTY PUBLIC LIBRARY, 223 W Washington, 46714. Tel 219-824-1612. *Dir* Charles N Joray; *ILL* Doris Wolf; *Ref* Babara Elliott; *Media* Ursula Kirchhoff; *Tech Serv & Cat* Kathryn Dotterer; *Commun Servs & Bkmobile Coordr* Margaret Hamilton. Staff 13 (prof 4, cler 9)
Founded 1902. Pop served 23,644; Circ 124,416
1978 Inc $262,928 (incl County funding). Exp $46,837, Bks $29,132, Per $4,183, Bd $900, Micro $2063, AV $10,558; Sal $105,788 (prof $46,060, cler $59,728)
Library Holdings: Bk titles 58,000, vols 63,919; Per sub 179, vols bd 900; Micro — Fiche 2750, reels 328; AV — Rec, Flm, Art repro. VF 16
Special Collections: Oral History

idea of the layout of governments and the information they contain.

Your local government, no matter how small, has a piece of printed material that outlines its form, describes and lists various agencies, and gives other basic information about your community. In some places, similar or better material will be available from a local League of Women Voters, so check with that organization too.

Cities and larger municipalities have extensive official directories, which contain specific information, including the names and numbers of bureau chiefs. In New York, the *Official Directory*, called "The Little Green Book" is the directory which lists (with telephone numbers) all city, state, and federal agencies with offices in the city. It is published each year and costs about three dollars.

Each state government also puts out a *Legislative Yearbook* or other manual describing itself, listing state representatives and heads of departments, giving information about salary scales, laws that govern state agencies, publications that are available, and so forth. You may want your own copy, depending on the kind of work you do. Your local library will have a copy.

No matter what your information needs are, though, you should have one of the directories that gives information about the U.S. Government and its parts. (See Chapter Seven for a thorough treatment of the federal government as an information resource.) The best is the *United States Government Manual,* published by the U.S. National Archives and Records Service (Washington: Government Printing Office, 1935 to date). It lists divisions and members of all branches of the government, includes all departments, agencies, and boards, and is indexed by name, subject, and agency. It comes out annually and is available from the Superintendent of Documents, U.S. General Printing Office, Washington, D.C. 20402, for about $6.50. (Again, if your city has a Federal Bookstore, you can probably get a copy there.) Another useful guide on matters federal is the *Official Congressional Directory* (Washington: Government Printing Office, 1809 to date), also a yearly publication. It gives facts on all congresspersons and officials, state by state, as well as committee structures and memberships, plus members of all commissions. A popular trade alternative to this book is the paperback *Almanac of American Politics, 1978,* by Michael Barone, Grant Ujifusa, and Douglas Matthews (New York: E. P. Dutton & Co., 1980).

You need a basic outline of the countries of the world, their locations, economies, population, types of governments. The best is the *Statesman's Year-book* (London: Macmillan, 1864 to date), published each year. It is a reliable and easy-to-use resource; it is a great argument settler as well.

Lastly, three essential information aids for your bookshelf are the catalogs of the Gale Research Company, the H. W. Wilson Company, and the R. R. Bowker Company. They are the major publishers of directories, guides, dictionaries and other reference books. By simply having their catalogs on hand, you'll soon become familiar with *what is out there* in the way of reference materials. It is better than having a listing of the reference books available at your library. The catalogs list books both by titles and subject and include such gems as the *National Directory of Newsletters and Reporting Services,* the *Reference Guide for Consumers,* and *Who's Who in Saudi Arabia.* You may want to buy one of their books one day. For the time being, it's enough to know what exists and can be requested at many libraries. Write to: Gale Research Company, Book Tower, Detroit, Michigan 48226, Attention: Library Services Department; the H. W. Wilson Company, 950 University Avenue, Bronx, New York 10452; and R. R. Bowker Company, 1180 Avenue of the Americas, New York, New York 10019.

While you're assembling your collection of reference materials for home or office, make sure you keep a list of several key telephone numbers as well. Your list should include the following:

The reference room of your local library (public, private, college, or corporate)

Your Congressperson's local office (or home address if he or she has no district office)

Your state representative's (Assemblyperson and/or State Senator) office

The number of your local bookstore. Bookstores have copies of *Books in Print,* which lists by author, title, and subject all American books in print. In a pinch, you can call the bookstore merely to find out if there *is* a book on a given subject.

(212) 790-6161, which is the Ready-Reference number of the New York Public Library. No matter where you are, you can call during library hours for the answer to a specific question. A researcher will either call you back with the information (if you live in New York City) or you can arrange to call him or her back later. The NYPL has now provided an after-hours service as well. Library-on-Call researchers will spend up to five minutes handling any one query during these hours: Monday–Thursday, 5-11 PM; Saturday, 10 AM -6 PM; and Sunday, 1-5 PM. You can dial free from anywhere in New York City (212) 780-7817 or Westchester County (914)682-8360. All ready-reference queries, except legal and medical problems, may be called in.

The number(s) of any reference service provided by newspapers in your community. Call your papers to see if they offer such service. Many do.

The number of the *National Union Catalog* if one exists in your community. A large local library may have such a number, through which you can find out whether that library has a specific book, which branch has copies of it, or the name of the nearest library owning the work. (You can then obtain the material through an interlibrary loan initiated by your librarian on your behalf.)

With these basics on your bookshelf you can begin almost any kind of information search. There are certainly other reference books worth having, depending on your job and areas of interests (see the Appendix for recommendations for your Researchers' Bookshelf by subject interest). But these are the essentials. You should not be without them, as they will start you off comfortably in the direction of finding out what you want to know.

3

finding experts

An expert can be merely a friend whose job (or interests) means he or she has certain kinds of information (the names of Hitchcock movies, for instance) which may one day be of value to you. One has no difficulty in asking a friend for information or leads; the stumbling block is to think of that friend as an "expert" in the first place.

Another kind of expert is the reference librarian, whom you find in libraries of all sizes and specialties — public, school, corporate, private. Reference librarians don't know very much about any one subject (besides libraries) but they are good leads to sources for the information you need. Their area of expertise is knowing exactly what material is in their collections and then connecting that knowledge with the question you are asking. A good librarian also knows how to help you ask the question better, but the asking remains your responsibility nonetheless. Chapter Five will consider how to find and use librarians.

SPECIALIZED PERSONS

Real experts, however, are specialized persons whom you probably do *not* know (or may not know of, even), whose jobs or avocations make them the sources to reach.

Assume, first, that the information you want is a fact or "quick" answer and that you cannot find the answer in a source at arm's length. (You have checked your dictionary, encyclopedia, and almanac, as well as your private collection of books and files.) Do you know anybody who might know of somebody who knows? Remember, all you're looking for is the name of a reachable source. If your question is very specific and one that falls under the heading of an almanac-type query, your first step should be to call a ready-reference number (library or newspaper), if one is in your community. Try your library first, asking for "ready reference" or merely stating your question to whomever answers the telephone. Your question must be specific — the number of barrels of crude oil pumped in Iran last year; the population of Santiago; etc. — and don't worry that it seems far-fetched. Ready-reference researchers get questions far more unusual than yours will be. What they are not equipped to handle is the caller who says, "I want some information about oil. What do you have available?" (That requires a different approach, explored in Chapter Five.)

The very best place to go for the name of an expert with whom you can get in touch quickly is the *Encyclopedia of Associations,* 13th ed., Volume 1 (Detroit: Gale Research Company, 1979). If I had to choose one reference book to own, other than a dictionary, it would be this work. The *Encyclopedia* will get you off on a running start towards finding out anything, from the scientific to the trivial. I have been told by professional business research consultants that when they can't think of the perfect source to go to on a project, they go directly to the *Encyclopedia of Associations* and begin calling around for source ideas. The book is not inexpensive (around $80 for Volume I, which is the only one you need), but if your job requires that you often hunt down information in varying fields, you ought to invest in this volume as a necessary expense of doing your business. In any case, your library probably will have a copy in its reference room.

The *Encyclopedia* lists thousands of national organizations, which are divided up into sections by type of organization. ("Trade, Business and Commercial Organization" is the largest section; "Scientific, Engineering and Technical Organizations" is another.) Within each section, the organizations are listed alphabetically by name, but an index in the back of the book lists them all by subject, key-word, and proper name. Each entry gives the location of the organization, telephone numbers, names of officers, membership size, purpose, function, committees, names of publications, and times of meeting.

★2146★
INTERNATIONAL ASSOCIATION OF INDEPENDENT PRODUCERS
(Motion Picture) (IAIP)
P.O. Box 1933   Phone: (202) 638-5595
Washington, DC 20013   Dr. E. Von Rothkirch, Exec.Dir.
Founded: 1954. **Members:** 1800. **Staff:** 1. Persons and firms associated
with all phases of the motion picture and recording industry. To facilitate
exchange of equipment, information, and personnel between independent film
producers and others in the areas of motion picture and recording production,
equipment manufacture, public relations, and accreditation. Sponsors
scholarships and on-the-job training and promotes an apprentice program in
the industry. Seeks to develop indigenous industry in areas where none has
existed. Maintains placement service. Library of 2400 volumes includes data
on production and direction of films and technical materials on operation and
manufacture of equipment. Sponsors 3-day seminars in U.S. and abroad. Holds
eight regional U.S. workshops, four European workshops, two Asian workshops
and one Latin American workshop. **Publications:** (1) Newsletter, 8/year; (2)
Communication Arts International, quarterly; (3) Film and Recording
Production, annual. **Formerly:** (1965) International Alliance of Film Producers.
Convention/ Meeting: annual - always September. 1981 Berlin, West
Germany; 1982 Veletta, Malta.

★2147★
INTERNATIONAL QUORUM OF **MOTION PICTURE** PRODUCERS (IQ)
P.O. Box 395   Phone: (703) 281-4508
Oakton, VA 22124   Barbara Legg, Exec. Sec.
Founded: 1966. **Members:** 125. Non-theatrical motion picture production
companies specializing in films for industry, government and television. "To
assist in the exchange of ideas, information and understanding among
members; to broaden the horizon of each member through affiliation with
member-producers located strategically around the world; to raise the
professional standards of non-theatrical motion pictures by examples of
excellence; to share among members new concepts and technology for the
betterment of motion pictures; to exchange information on personnel,
equipment and markets for the good of all members; to provide members with
information on photography and other conditions in each area; and to simplify
and render more productive the operations of its members." **Publications:** (1)
Quorum Quotes, quarterly; (2) IQ Directory, annual. **Convention/ Meeting:**
annual.

Figure 3-1. From the *Encyclopedia of Associations,* 14th edition.
Reprinted with permission of Gale Research Company. Copyright ©
1980 Gale Research Company.

If, for example, you are looking for information
about film distribution in motion picture theaters, you might
check "film" or "motion picture" in the index, or you could go
directly to the "Trade, Business and Commercial Organizations"
section and look up "Motion picture" alphabetically there.
Under that category you'll find entries for 10 to 12 organizations who focus on film activities, from the Film Producers

Association of New York to the National Association of Theatre Owners. When you read the detailed descriptions of their activities, you'll soon see which source offers you the best route to the information you want.

Researchers prize the *Encyclopedia* because the organizations listed therein are in the business of giving out information. They will handle informal, over-the-telephone requests. They know their fields well enough to help you define the search you're on. And they are usually eager to help you learn more about their areas of expertise and interest. That fact alone makes them better resources than many experts who may work within a given field but whose jobs have nothing to do with *communicating* information from their field to those outside.

Another valuable source on experts is the *Research Centers Directory*, 6th ed., (Detroit: Gale Research Company, 1979) and its updated supplements *New Research Centers*. These list over 5,000 university-related and other nonprofit research programs. Entries detail subject covered, method of funding, size and location of project, extent of library, and, most important, the names and numbers of personnel, including names of librarians. The *Directory* is particularly helpful if the information you seek is highly specialized or scientific — there are lengthy sections on all branches of the sciences and engineering, from archeology to nuclear physics.

An even more specialized source for scientific information is the federal government's *A Directory of Information Resources in the United States (Scientific)*, (Washington: Library of Congress, 1971) published by the Science and Technology Division of the National Referral Center. Though somewhat out of date by now, the information can be helpful nonetheless. The book details all government services and publications in the field and lets you know who will answer inquiries and what procedures to follow in making them.

Other directories of experts provide more specialized lists: *Thomas' Register of American Manufacturers* (New York: Thomas Publishing Company, Inc., 1905 to date) and *Poor's Register of Corporations, Directors, and Executives* (New York: Standard & Poor's Corporation, 1928 to date) are the two standard sources found in the world of business and finance. New editions of each are issued annually.

There are thousands more, a directory for practically any profession or hobby you can name. The *U.S. Directory of Marine Scientists; Directory of Historical Societies and Agencies; Washington Women: A Directory of Women and Women's Organizations in the National Capitol.* The list is huge. If your information searches tend to fall within one or two subject areas, you should obtain the directories that relate to those fields. See the Appendix for lists of selected works, including directories, by field or subject interest.

With such an abundance of directories, it was only a matter of time before someone came up with the idea of compiling a directory of directories. Two enterprising publishers have done just that. Bernard Klein is the editor of *Guide to American Directories*, 10th ed. (Coral Springs, Fla: B. Klein Publications, 1978), which annotates listings of over 6000 business, professional, and special-interest directories, indexed by subject-title. The other rich lode in the Directory of Directories line is the periodical *Directory Information Service* (Detroit: Gale Research, six times a year), which has year-end cumulative subject and title indexes. The index will direct you to one or more issues, where descriptions of directories in your subject field can be found. In the subject index under "Lawyers", for instance, there are over 60 entries, from the *Directory of Law Teachers* and the *Directory of Women Law Graduates and Attorneys in the USA* to such standard works as *Martindale-Hubbell Law Directory*. The directories are described in great detail. Much of the material in Directory Information Service is now also available in a one-volume work, the recently published *Directory of Directories* (Detroit: Gale Research Company, 1980).

These three expert resources — *Encyclopedia of Associations*, the *Research Centers Directory*, and one of the Directory-of-Directories works — will be in most medium-size

★ 4959 ★
CENTER FOR MIGRATION STUDIES
209 Flagg Place
Staten Island, New York 10304   Phone: 212-351-8800
Dr. Sylvan M. Tomasi, Director   Founded: 1964

Independent nonprofit research organization with its own board of control.
Supported by research grants. Staff: 5 research professionals, 21 supporting
professionals, 3 others.

Principal fields of research: Sociological, demographic, historical, pastoral
and legislative aspects of human migration movements and ethnic group
relations, including studies about people on the move in North American
and other countries. Operates in collaboration with Centro Studi Emigrazione
in Rome, Italy, and Centro do Estudos Migratorios in Sao Paulo, Brazil.

Research results published in professional journals, monographs, books and
pamphlets. Publication: INTERNATIONAL MIGRATION REVIEW
(quarterly) and MIGRATION TODAY (bimonthly). Holds intermittent conferences for professionals and nonprofessionals from groups under study.
Maintains a reference library and immigration archives which are available to
researchers by permission.

★ 4960 ★
CENTER FOR NEO-HELLENIC STUDIES
1010 West 22nd Street
Austin, Texas 78705   Phone: 512-477-5526
E.G. Arnakis, Acting Director   Founded: 1965

Independent nonprofit research organization located at University of Texas
but with its own board of trustees. Supported by patrons, benefactors and
trustees.

Prncipal fields of research: Greek history and culture from thirteenth to
twentieth century, including studies in modern Greek literature and translation of literary works, also publication of old travel books and writings
of Americans who took part in Greek War of Independence. Awards annual
prizes for modern Greek literature in the United States and studies on modern
Greece and the Greek-American community.

Research result published in books and professional journals. Publications:
BULLETIN since 1966 and NEO-HELLENIKA since 1970.

Figure 3-2. From the *Research Centers Directory,* 6th edition. Reprinted
with permission of Gale Research Company. Copyright © 1979 Gale
Research Company.

42

Figure 3-3. From *Guide to American Directories,* 11/E.
Reprinted with permission from B. Klein Publications.
Copyright © 1980 B. Klein Publications, Coral Springs,
Florida 33065.

libraries. Large public libraries may have one copy in their
reference rooms and another in their business or science divisions. Ask at the librarian's desk before searching the shelves. A
good first-time use of these resources would be to draw up a list
(with names and numbers) of the ten or fifteen associations,
research centers, and directories that seem to relate to your line
of work. You can either go about obtaining the directories right
away or merely keep the list, on cards or in a notebook, at your
desk for future reference. You'll have reduced the chances of
your ever again muttering "I wonder where I could find someone who knows . . . "

This is perhaps the place to mention *Who's Who* in
all its myriad forms. They are not the books to go to when you
need an expert but know only the field or subject of expertise.
Most of the *Who's Who* volumes are generalized works (*Who's
Who in America; Who's Who in Business and Industry; Who's
Who in the Arts*) that will give you lots of information about
particular individuals provided that you already know the individuals' names. As the books list persons alphabetically by
names only, they will not help you find an expert whose name
you don't already know. I use them to tell me the whereabouts

of an already well-known person or to fill me in on that person's background. But by then the hardest part of the search is done, I know who it is I'm trying to locate. Don't waste time thumbing through these books if you are still searching for a name. A useful guide called *Who Knows — And What, Among Authorities-Experts and the Specially Informed* (Chicago: Marquis Who's Who, Inc., 1954) may be in your library. Experts are listed alphabetically by name but there is a subject index as well. However, the work has not been revised since 1954, which means you may have difficulty in locating many of the experts cited. Still, the opportunity to find the one person in America who is an authority of "Albany River–history" is not to be discarded lightly. Use it if you can as a back-up resource.

EXPERTS IN THE GOVERNMENT

The greatest gaggle of experts living in any one place in America, (perhaps in the world) is to be found in Washington, D.C. They are the people who work for the federal government, and many of them are valuable and little-known information resources. There are several ways to find the right experts there for your information searches.

The quickest way to find an expert in the government on any subject is to call the Federal Information Center of the Government Services Administration (7th and D Street, S.W., Washington, D.C. 20407) at (202) 755–8669. You can write if you wish, but why waste time. Ask them anything. Depending on the depth of the information you need, the center's staff will refer you to specific agencies, departments, and even specific individuals. A recent call for vaguely worded information on the subject of solar energy, for example, provided me with the names of three persons at the Department of Energy's National Solar Heating and Cooling Information Center. It would have taken me a much longer time to come up with that name by scanning my copy of the *Government Manual.*

If you have a specific question for which no local source was able to provide an answer, call on the government. Try the National Referral Center at the Library of Congress. (See Chapter Five for more on this valuable resource.) The center will give you the names of organizations or study groups currently working on the subject you're interested in.

Or try the Bureau of the Census in the U.S. Department of Commerce. If the information you need is statistical or at all quantifiable (how many, how much), this is a fine place to go. Forget the notion that the census comes out only once in ten years and is therefore "old" data. The Bureau is a full-time research organization, running weekly and monthly surveys on every subject category imaginable (from age and sex, to aliens, fertility, and religion). Write for the Bureau's "Telephone Contacts for Data Users," which lists the names and telephone numbers of the individual analysts handling each subject. The sheet is available for $4 from Subscriber Services Section, Bureau of the Census, Washington, D.C. 20233.

Or try the Department of Commerce's Office of the Ombudsman, which can refer you to specialists in most areas of business, industry, and trade. The office uses over one hundred analysts to research specific industries, and in conducting their research they work with private trade and industry associations. Thus, an inquiry to the office can not only get you the names of department experts to speak with but also names of the department's own outside experts, people whom you wouldn't be able to find without the referral. Contact the Office of the Ombudsman, Bureau of Domestic Business Development, Industry and Trade Administration, U.S. Department of Commerce, Washington, D.C. 20230. (202)377-3176.

Or try the Department of Agriculture. If the information you seek is economic and in any way related to commodities, food, or agriculture (don't think merely "farming" — it's much larger than that), get in touch with the Economics, Statistics and Cooperative Service [Department of Agriculture, Washington, D.C. 20250. (202) 447-4230] and tell them about your search. Their analysts can answer specific questions, give you background and bibliographic material, and may even spend time with you in person to help you obtain a complete grasp of your subject.

Or call your elected representative. If your search concerns a federal law or program, contact your congressperson (always likely to be more accessible than your senator), who may have a home office in addition to his or her Washington one. Ask for the legislative assistant and describe to that person the information you're seeking. Be sure to mention also the purpose for which you're doing the research, which will give the assistant an indication of your time pressures and the level of detail you're working with. Some offices will ask that you put your request in writing, but many will handle specific information questions over the telephone. Your congressperson is also your valuable link to many of the research services of the Library of Congress. These are services you would not be able to use on your own. See Chapter Five for a description of these and how to use them by going through your elected representative.

If you're not sure which agency, or which person to call in the government, pick up that essential aid, the *United States Government Manual* (which you should buy right now if you don't already have it). Read through the descriptions of the various agencies if you really can't think of the one that might relate to your subject. Most government agencies have at least one department that performs research functions. Under an agency's listing you'll find a division detailed in terms such as, "develops . . . a program of economic, statistical, and other . . . research analysis and information related to . . . " or similar governmentese. In that department are the people you want to start with. Call the agency, ask for that department, then ask for the analyst (everyone's an "analyst" in such departments) who works on ___. Buried among books, papers and computer terminals as they are likely to be all day, these experts are often more than willing to talk to a friendly voice seeking information on their specialties. If no such description or department can be found within the agency's listing, go back to square one, which is that agency's Public Affairs or Public Information Office.

Like congresspersons, government agency officials may require that you put your information request in writing. This is not because it's actually required, but often because the official doesn't know offhand who the proper person is to handle your question. Once he or she receives a letter, it can be "bucked" to a number of people within or outside that agency. You may eventually be put in touch with the right source, but it's going to take several weeks via this route. Writing letters to anyone in the government ranks near the bottom of the information-getting scale. If you can train yourself to think of the telephone as the best, most natural way to get information from anyone about any subject, you'll be surprised how often you'll be able to avoid letter-writing, even in cases where it's supposedly "required."

FINDING OUT WHO'S AN EXPERT

If you can't find an expert by using any of the previously described resources, you must begin at the beginning. The beginning of an expert-hunt is the subject itself, and you had better first learn the basics of your subject (you'll need them to interview an expert later, anyway).

Encyclopedias give basic information, but they're apt to be too generalized for your purpose here, which is to find the names of living, reachable persons. Newspaper and magazine articles are a better bet. Go first to the *Readers' Guide to Periodical Literature* (New York: the H. W. Wilson Company, semimonthly and monthly), which every library will have. See Chapter Six for details on this source. Begin with the most recent issue and work your way back to the large yearly volumes, looking under your subject's heading. What you're after are articles that appeared in the general newsweeklies: *Time, Newsweek, U.S. News and World Report.* Your library is more likely to have those periodicals than smaller magazines; and the newsweeklies take a "summarizing" approach to most subjects. There will be at least one paragraph that gives a capsulized view of the topic, quotes one or two experts in the field, and may include the name of the standard work on the subject if there is one. At the very least you'll come away with an idea of the subject headings or topics that make up your subject; you'll then be in a position to approach the *Encyclopedia of Associations,* specific directories, or other resources described earlier. Write down three or four key-word topics that you garner from reading these articles. Then look for them in the indexes of the specialized reference books.

The next square-one resource to consult is the *New York Times Index* (New York: New York Times, 1913 to date). These large red volumes should be in your library's reference room. Again, start with the most recent volumes, and work backwards. In the case of the *New York Times,* this approach is essential, as you'll want to avoid having to use microfilm if you can. (Issues other than those most recent are stored on microfilm in most libraries.) The *New York Times Index* is even more helpful than the *Readers' Guide,* since under each subject heading you find not only an article title but a concise outline of the article. Sometimes, names of authorities and sources will crop up here and you'll be able to circumvent having to read the original column.

If all these sources yield small results, you're going to have to dig deep indeed, consulting other indexes and the library's card catalog to direct you to books and articles. Again, try the most recently published ones first, which you will then read to cull for names of experts. Even if you must take this route, however, there are shortcuts to note.

Once you've located a book on your subject, before reading it, look at the author's introduction or acknowledgements page. "I'd like to thank so-and-so . . . " can be a fruitful direction pointer for you. The thank-you's will occasionally give clues as to the whereabouts of the expert; "Mary Smith of the Morgan Library." After all, if the author drew on the expertise of these individuals, why can't you? Footnotes — whether these are on the pages themselves as part of the running text or in a separate section at the back of the book — are other sites where authors divulge who helped them and with what kinds of information. And as another last resort, there is the author. Authors of nonfiction books almost always have notes or card files on the sources they consulted. It is not beyond reason that an author might share this information with you. Locate the author (*Who's Who, Contemporary Authors,* through his or her publisher — see the following pages for more hints on locating people) and explain what you're looking for and why. The chances are good that the author will consider helping you in your search. After all, he or she had to start at just such a point, too.

GETTING IN TOUCH WITH EXPERTS

You want to get in touch with a perfect stranger. You know the person's name and perhaps have some general idea of the expert's specialty (you wouldn't be trying to get information from an expert unless you knew what kinds of information he or she would be likely to have). You might know, for instance, that he's a doctor, she's a lawyer, he's an architect, and nothing more. That's enough to start you on your way towards obtaining an address and telephone number.

If there's any reason to think the expert lives in your city, consult the telephone directory. Not all notables have unlisted numbers, and this resource is too close to your arm to overlook.

Who's Who in America (Chicago: Marquis Who's Who, Inc., 1899 to date) and all the *Who's Who* books (many of these are included by subject listing of sources in the Appendix) give addresses and sometimes telephone numbers at the end of each entry. The address given may be for the person's office, agent, or publisher, or it may be a home address. *Who's Who* also includes club membership in its entries, and that may prove a quicker way to reach someone than the more formal business approach. Note the name and address of any club to which your expert belongs. For one thing, it will provide a clue as to the city in which he or she lives, enabling you to call "information" for that town. If you suspect your quarry is sufficiently well known in his or her field to appear in a *Who's Who*, call your librarian, and ask for the address given at the end of the entry or the names of clubs listed. You need not know the specific *Who's Who* to go to, but can merely tell the librarian you want an address for so-and-so, the painter or writer or scientist, or whatever is the field. A good librarian will know which directories to consult. Another good source for locating known experts is the *Directory of American Scholars,* 7th ed. (New York: R. R. Bowker Company, 1978). This four-volume work contains profiles of over 40,000 persons, arranged by field. Scholars working in History; English, Speech and Drama; Linguistics, Philosophy, Religion, and Law are listed here, with one overall alphabetical index to all four volumes. *Contemporary Authors* (Detroit: Gale Research Co., 1962 to date) is another direction-pointer to persons whose names you know.

If your expert is less well-known than a *Who's Who* entrant, proceed on the assumption that he or she has written a book. That may not turn out to be the case, but if it is, this will be the easiest next step to take in finding the person. Call the library. (Pick a small library for these calls if you can. A librarian there will be more likely to do this kind of checking for you than will a reference desk librarian in a large unit.) Ask the librarian to look in the card catalogue under the expert's name for the name and city of that person's publisher. If time is not a stringent requirement, you can write to your expert, sending the letter to the publisher with "please forward" on its envelope. If you are really pressed for time, call the publisher and ask to speak to the editor who handles your expert's books. Explain why you want to reach the writer and ask how you might do that most speedily. A sympathetic and trusting editor

SYRETT, DAVID, b White Plains, NY, Jan 8, 39; m 62; c 3. BRITISH EIGHTEENTH CENTURY NAVAL HISTORY. Educ: Columbia Univ, BA, 61, MA, 64; Univ London, PhD (hist), 66. Prof Exp: Asst prof, 66-71, ASSOC PROF HIST, QUEENS COL, NY, 71- Mem: Navy Rec Soc, Eng; Royal Hist Soc; Soc Nautical Res; AHA. Res: British naval history in the 18th century. Publ: Auth, Shipping and the American War, Univ London, 70; Siege and Capture of Havana, Navy Rec Soc, 70. Add: Dept of Hist Queens Col Flushing NY 11367

SYRETT, HAROLD COFFIN, b New York, NY, Oct 22, 13; m 37; c 3. HISTORY. Educ: Wesleyan Univ, AB, 35; Columbia Univ, MA, 38, PhD, 44. Prof Exp: Teacher, Harvey Sch, 36-39; instr Am hist, Univ Maine, 41; from instr to prof, Columbia Univ, 41-61; prof hist & dir grad studies, Queens Col, NY, 61-62, dean fac, 62-65; dean grad studies, State Univ NY, 65-66, vchancellor, 66-67; PROF HIST, GRAD CTR, CITY UNIV NEW YORK, 69- Concurrent Pos: Ed, Papers of Alexander Hamilton, 55-; pres, Brooklyn Col, 68- Mem: AHA; Orgn Am Historians. Res: American history, 1775-1800, 1865-1900. Publ: Auth, Andrew Jackson; The City of Brooklyn, 1865-1898; coauth, History of the American People. Add: Box 136 RD 1 Craryville NY 12521

Figure 3-4. From the *Directory of American Scholars,* Seventh edition. Reprinted with permission of R. R. Bowker Company. Copyright © 1979 by Xerox Corporation.

may give you the address. More likely, he or she will promise to pass on your letter quickly.

Or you might try a university or college department as a source of an expert's whereabouts. If your expert is a biologist, for instance, call the biology department of a large school nearby, asking for the head of that department. You'll probably reach a secretary or graduate student assistant, but that's all you need, someone who will do the associative work and legwork for you. Be forthright about your dilemma: Ask if they have any clues as to how you should go about reaching the person. Tell them why you want to reach the person. Do they know where he or she teaches, works, does research? Or is there another teacher within their department who follows that specialty, who might have an idea? You will be surprised how people within a particular field manage to keep track of the whereabouts (and titles, honors, job changes, and promotions) of their colleagues.

Always think associatively about how to locate someone. If you must, write down whatever you know about the person — anything at all. Your list may suggest a new approach when previous ones have failed. You have to assume that the person you're looking for *has* a location — even hermits pick up their mail someplace — and thus it's merely a question of your narrowing down the possibilities to a particular state, town, job, club, street, and telephone number. You arrive there by finding a person who knows the person you're after; or finding a person who knows a person who knows the person. . . . If all the regular routes fail, be inventive. Try long shots. Look at the problem from a new angle.

I once had to locate Dom DiMaggio, the brother of Joe, for a television producer who was considering a dramatization of Joe's life. Assuming that the more famous DiMaggio would know where his brother was, I tried to reach Joe DiMaggio without going through the formal process of applying to his agent or secretary. I knew that Joe DiMaggio often appeared in television commercials for a New York bank. I called the bank and asked for the name of the advertising agency that prepared their commercials, then called that agency and asked for the person handling the bank's account. The account executive I reached had worked with DiMaggio for some time by then, and they were friends. He was sympathetic to my search, but to protect the DiMaggios, he asked that I put my request in writing. He would pass it on quickly. That was not quick enough for me, however. The only other shred of information I knew about the DiMaggios was that they were originally from San Francisco. I called "information" there and asked for a listing for Dom. There wasn't any, but there was one for DiMaggio's Restaurant. The restaurant, it devolved, was indeed owned by the family; the manager knew Dom well and knew how to reach him. It was, in the end, a quicker way to get to DiMaggio than the New York connection would have provided.

Occasionally, a truly far-fetched route pays off. On another assignment I needed information about an historical figure who died in the 1930s. Specifically, I wanted to find persons who had known him, who would themselves still be alive. I went to the major written work on my subject, a biography published forty years ago. The author's acknowledgment gave names and a few location hints on the sources he had used, but there was no way to figure out which of those sources were still alive. It seemed reasonable to me, though, that the author might have kept his notes or would recall the ages and whereabouts of those sources. But the author had not written for some years and so was not himself listed in the usual directories that might contain an address or clue to his whereabouts. Even his former publisher had no address he could lay his hands on quickly. I went back to the book, this time looking at the author's introduction. I don't know why or when the practice began, but authors sometimes sign their introductions with the date, then the place from which they're writing. This particular introduction was signed from a small town in upstate New York. Perhaps my author had retired there? He had, indeed, and was listed with "information" for that town. One moral of this story is that research is at least part luck; the other is that you never get the chance to be lucky if you don't try the apparent wild goose chase.

Should there be no directory that comes to mind, no angle you can create to get you started on the telephone, no helpful librarian, and no outside source who will know what you're talking about — then you have no recourse but to go to the library yourself and dig into the familiar reference materials mentioned previously: the *Readers' Guide;* the *New York Times Index;* and the others. None of these will provide you with your expert's address, but they may, through orderly checking, give you the names of other persons who might know how to reach him or her. If a magazine article has ever been written on your expert, find out who wrote it or did the research for it. If your expert's name is mentioned in a newspaper article, note the date and page and call that paper. Their dead-articles files may contain clues. If you know the expert's field, get in touch with several of the national associations in that area and ask them for clues. Or find the names of directories that pertain to that field and call those who publish them. Try asking outright if your expert is listed in their directory.

As you go through these and all leads, be sure you write down any new shred of information you collect about your quarry. Knowing where someone went to school, for instance, can lead you to him or her, through an alumnae (alumni) office's mailing list. The more you know about someone, the more avenues you'll have to explore in finding them. One avenue will work if you are persistent and perhaps a little bit creative. But don't ever give up trying to locate a person who exists. *Everyone* is somewhere.

4

getting
information
from
experts

Once you've found your first "expert," you must interview him or her for information. An interview need not be a formal, prearranged or in-person discussion. An interview is any verbal contact with a source, either by telephone or in person.

You should learn to determine when the telephone is the better route to information and when the personal interview is preferable. Start with the assumption that the telephone is the better way to go, unless you're writing for publication and the expert is either to be the subject of the piece or the major quoted source used. The telephone takes less time, but even more importantly, the dynamics of asking for information are less complex on the telephone and thus more apt to yield results.

When you ask for information, whether it's for one or two facts or lengthier material, you become part of the search equation. How you speak, how you look, what you say — these are all parts of the asking. Much of the first few minutes in an in-person interview is nonverbal communication. Shrugs, facial expression, posture, voice tone, how you look, dress, move, speak — these all give indications of what you're seeking. These aspects will to some extent influence the outcome of your search as the interviewee responds to the nonverbal clues. It may work to your advantage or it may not.

On the telephone, there are fewer nonverbal messages to which one responds. Your phrasing and voice tone are present, of course, but the person on the other end will hear the content of your question and not much more. You're apt to be helped more quickly and more accurately.

There are times, however, when the information you seek is such that a source may be hesitant to part with it.

Persuasion is called for here, and you stand a better chance if you arrange to see the person. It's much easier to say, "I can't help you" on the telephone. If you really need the information and this is the best source to go to, take the time to set up an interview.

The personal interview is also called for if the information you seek is lengthy and/or complex. This is especially true if you're interviewing someone in order to get a general knowledge of the subject (you should brief yourself first through books and articles, but that's not always possible and you can sometimes get away with not having done so). Before you start bombarding someone with numerous questions over the telephone, think to yourself: Is this person used to being asked for information in this way? A person who handles information requests daily (someone who works for a polling firm, a government information office, or with statistics) is probably used to answering questions over the telephone, even if the questions turn out to be lengthy and detailed. But someone whose job is analytical or is conducted at a more measured pace — or certainly someone in a high-titled position — is not used to the brusque approach that the telephone conveys. This source will provide information more readily in the more intimate and prearranged setting of the personal interview. A few seconds of the telephone conversation will indicate whether this person ought to be seen either because of his or her reticence on the telephone or because the extent of his or her knowledge warrants more time spent.

THE TELEPHONE INTERVIEW

We were all taught how to use the telephone. "Hello, this is Nancy Jones speaking, is Mr. Smith there?" The researcher's call is not very different. You must identify both yourself and the person with whom you wish to speak.

Identifying yourself means more than giving your name. In most cases the person you're calling will want to know

why you need the information you say you need. Questions fly-
ing through the mind of the person on the other end of the line
include: Who are you? What do you do for a living? Whom do
you work for? Is my name going to be used? Am I going to be
asked for information I don't have or shouldn't give? Am I
going to get in trouble? If you force the interviewee to articulate any of them because you've failed to anticipate his concerns, you won't get very far. You must identify yourself right
away, not merely as Nancy Jones but more specifically as a
nice person who is seeking help and poses no threat. "This is
Nancy Jones. I'm with such-and-such a company (or school). I'm
writing a report on ____ for ____ (name of publication, firm, or
whatever) is your best approach. It may also help to explain
how you came to be calling this person (I was given your name
by Bob Bradman in the Department of Agriculture or I saw
your name mentioned in an article in ____ Magazine). The more
detail you give about yourself the more you disarm the other
person's natural defenses.

     If you can't tell everything about who you are and
why you want the information you're seeking, then don't; but
don't lie. Face the fact that the vaguer you are about yourself,
the more suspicion (and less willingness to help) you'll arouse.
You should also realize that the ubiquitous "I'm doing research
for a school paper . . . " has been used so often to cover up the
real reasons why some persons seek information that it is often
received with doubt. If you're not a student, don't even attempt
it as an opening line, and if you are a student, you may not be
believed.

     You can identify yourself without telling what you
don't wish to reveal. Give your name and the name of your
firm (I'm Nancy Jones, and I work for Plymouth Corporation,
and I'd like to speak with someone who might know about
____"). This lets the other person know something about you
without really giving away very much. Of course, if your firm's
name is the Plymouth Collection Agency or the Plymouth
Executive Search Firm, that's another matter entirely.

     But in most instances, there's nothing to hide, and
you're better off specifying as much as possible about yourself

and your query. If you're writing an article, then say for whom. Don't wait for the person on the other end to have to ask. The information you give about yourself and what you do also helps to define your query; and that helps the interviewee to help you better.

Sometimes, a person doing research may not want to divulge his or her purpose. A researcher in an executive search firm (they're known as "head hunters" to many companies whose talented employees they hire away) wanted to obtain information on the background of a high-level officer in a government agency. There was no "official" biography available, so the searcher had to think of a way to acquire a personal resume without having to say "I work for an executive search firm that is thinking of luring this fellow away from his present job to one with our client." No suitable way surfaced and, in the end, the searcher called the job candidate's secretary and said simply "This is Tom Brown with the Reynolds Company (that is, gave his firm's actual name) in New York. We've been asked to come up with the names of persons working in ____ field and I'd like to obtain a copy of Mr. Brayard's background information sheet or resume." He received it the next day. And who knows *what* the secretary thought, whether she asked her boss for permission, or anything else. Sometimes a search is easier than it seems to the searcher.

After identifying yourself and your search, if you hear a pause or suspect reticence on the other end of the line, a good question is, "Is this a convenient time to ask you about this or would you rather I call back later?" This gives the person something definite to answer (don't forget: he or she is thinking all those suspicious thoughts as well as trying to understand what you want) and gives him or her a graceful way out if time is needed to pull together the information you want. That way, he or she doesn't have to be the one to say, "I'm not sure where the information is right now — I saw it somewhere — maybe it's in my file — " or anything else that makes him sound ill-prepared and inefficient at his job. He can simply respond, "Well, I am busy right now, suppose you call back at two or three. I'll have it then." But be sure that you pinpoint a definite time at which you'll call, and that you do call at that time.

If the person says immediately that he or she can't help you, make sure you ask "Do you know someone I might call who would have this information?" NEVER HANG UP WITHOUT ASKING FOR THE NAME OF ANOTHER SOURCE. That is a cardinal rule of research. Even people who can't or don't want to help you with information will usually be willing to suggest another source — it shows that they do know *something!*

Be friendly on the telephone; courteous, and lively, too. If your voice communicates that you're interested in your search, glad you reached the person you did, and are interested in who they are and what they know, you'll get more information. Don't be excessively formal or stilted in your speech — there's nothing wrong with admitting "You know, I'm having a devil of a time trying to understand why *(specific).*" It tells the other person that you're fallible and not likely to be judging them on how well they do their job.

Don't feign dumbness or won't-you-help-poor-little-me-out, especially if you're a woman. It doesn't work. The answers you'll get (if any) will be imprecise and insufficient. No one wants to be asked stupid questions by a stupid person. If you suspect that your voice sounds younger and more inexperienced than you are — many women have felt this — then work into the conversation a fact or piece of information that you know which relates to your search. "I know the Health Act of 1974 deals with this, but what I'd really like to know is what other legislation is coming up on this subject . . . " or a similar insert, lets the other person know that you've been doing your own research and aren't just counting on him or her to do all your work for you. It also accords that person's job and expertise more respect.

Assume that the person you're talking to is going to be able to help you. (This is another corollary of the researcher's basic rule, stressed throughout this book: Assume the Information You Want Is There.) If you sound optimistic about your search, it will rub off on others, and they'll be more likely to believe that, indeed, they *can* help you after all.

Take notes, even on a telephone interview, and even if the person was not helpful. At the very least, you should always record the name and number of the person you called and the date and time of call. That person may turn out to be a source worth considering on another search or, at worst, you ought to be sure you never bother him or her again (if that's what you gleaned from the conversation). If your conversation was lengthy, your notes may be a combination of shorthand, abbreviations, key words, and doodles. Right after you hang up is the time to sit down and write up your notes in a coherent form. You think you'll remember later what transpired by just looking at your original notes, but you won't. Don't even question this axiom; make yourself transcribe right away.

Finally, don't forget the thank you. If it's been a lengthy conversation, or the person has been of enormous help, or is going to be, or is someone you may want to call on again — write a short thank-you note. It can't hurt; and even if it doesn't help you, it'll help the next researcher who reaches that person.

THE PERSONAL INTERVIEW

You'll usually want to call first to make an appointment for an interview. If the person you want to see is a public figure (or sometimes a very busy private one), the purpose of your call is to find out the correct procedure to follow in requesting an interview. A letter will probably be required.

Ask the subject's secretary or assistant — again, after you've said who you are, what your research is on and for what purpose it's being done — "What is the best way for me to go about getting an interview with ____?" If the person you wish to interview does not live in your area, now is also the time to find out "Does ____ ever come to the (*where you live*) area or must the interview be done in (*where he or she lives*)?" You should also let the secretary know how much time you'll need for the interview. Unless yours is a very lengthy project and this subject is your major source, your interview should not run over an hour and a half.

Send a letter, no matter what the secretary said. In some cases (government and political figures, in particular) you'll be asked to do so, even if the person agreed to the interview on the telephone. Your letter should restate your request: It should say who you are, what your project is, what purpose it will serve, and how long the interview will take. If you don't have a firm date set yet for the interview, say at the end of your letter either, "I will call your office next week to make an appointment," or "I look forward to hearing from you as to a definite time when I might speak with you." If you haven't heard after two weeks, call the office.

To tape or not to tape? All things being equal, ask if you may tape. You get more information in a taped interview, because you are free to listen and think, instead of scribbling away furiously trying to get down names, places, key-words, etc. If the subject refuses to be taped, then of course you have no choice. Corporate and government officials do not like to be taped, in general. Sometimes, persons want you to have information but do not want it known that they gave it to you. Obviously, all such conversations are "off the record" and not taped.

For a short informal interview, where you know exactly what information you need and are not likely to get a long discourse on the subject, I think it's overbearing to come with equipment. But in all other cases, I'd do it, whether you feel uncomfortable with the machine, or whether your subject says he or she does. (People I've interviewed who said at first, "No, I don't mind, but it does make me feel uncomfortable," often forgot about the machine entirely as they warmed to their subject.) The important rule, if you do tape, is to be sure to tell your subject ahead of time that at any point you will turn off the machine if he or she wishes to say something off the record.

Bring enough tapes with you. The best cassettes

cover either a half-hour or forty-five minutes on each side; the longer ones get tangled up or just stop; the shorter ones make you worry throughout the interview that your tape is running out on you.

Before you leave for your interview, test your machine. Put in new batteries, even if you think the old ones are fine. Place the microphone (or console itself) on a table a few feet away from you (to simulate the distance it will be from your subject) and speak in a normal conversational tone. You want to make sure that the machine picks up moderate voice level while screening out other noises. When you walk into the room for the actual interview, look to see if there's an open window, then ask if you may close it. The best machine can't compete with the sounds of trucks and jackhammers.

Once you have tested your machine put in the cassette you'll be using for the interview and let it run for a few seconds. Sometimes the first few inches are not recordable. Remember this also when, in the interview, you turn the tape over. Run the new side a few seconds before continuing your questions. Record on the tape "This is June 7th, an interview with ____." Then you're ready to interview. Most machines either will beep or click noticeably when one side is finished. Even if your machine does, keep an eye out for its progress. If a side seems to be almost but not quite at its end and there's a natural pause in the conversation, don't wait. Stop your machine, write "one" or "A" on the side just taped, turn it over and continue.

Keep your used tapes, properly labeled, for a long time. They don't take up much room, and you never can tell when you might have to verify something that transpired or even the fact that the interview itself took place. And, for this reason, too, you don't want anything erased; so if you do not do your own transcribing, see that the person who is doing it is familiar with how your machine works, and will return all tapes to you.

In general, it is better to do your own transcribing

and to do it as soon after the interview as possible. You'll hear things you might have missed in the interview (because you were watching your machine perhaps), and you'll be able to call your subject for clarification while the interview is still fresh in his or her mind. You'll also be in a better position to figure out an apparently incoherent name or mumbled phrase than will a transcriber who was not present at the conversation. Whether you do the transcribing or not, make two copies of your interview transcript — one to store intact, the other for marking up, cutting, and/or pasting into a final report or article form.

Be prepared for the interview itself. Go into it having done homework about your expert and his or her field. Use biographical reference books to look the person up beforehand. (See Chapter Six and the Appendix for specific works to check.) Try the same books you might have used (cited in the previous chapter) to locate the expert in the first place. Or call the person's secretary and ask if there's any recent printed work on him or her. If you can't find any information on your person, be sure you've made at least some headway in your research on the person's field and specialty.

Have a list of questions drawn up before you go. You may use some, all, or none of them; but having them will make you feel more at ease, knowing you have them to fall back on when a previous question brings forth only a "yes" or "no" in response. But don't interrupt someone's train of thought in conversation, merely to insert one of your questions. You can always end the interview with a catchall, "I have several unrelated questions I meant to ask you."

Begin the interview with more generalized questions, then move toward specifics. No one wants to be grilled in an intense and rapid fashion. Try to design your first question as a friendly, large one — one that will require some time and thought in response. It will put both you and your expert at ease. Then you can get on to specifics, showing also that you know something about your interviewee's field. From that point on, the interview will roam all over the subject (and others), guided less by your plans and more by the dynamics of how you and the person talk to each other.

The fundamental determinant of whether you get the information you need from an interview will be whether you listened. It's simple, but cannot be overemphasized. One obtains more and better information by listening than by any other trick of interviewing. Forget about how you're doing, whether your machine is working, what your next question will be, or anything else that occupies the mind. Just listen to what is being said and respond to that. Sometimes, there's no response. Don't worry about pauses. They occur in all conversations; you're not supposed to have to cover them up with questions. If you are listening, you'll realize when something is being said that you don't understand. Ask for clarification. This applies to aspects of the subject being discussed but also to names and places. People in a particular field often speak of their colleagues as if everyone surely knows their names. Don't ever be hesitant to interrupt and ask, "What's his name? Where does he work? How could I reach him?" Now is also the time to get the correct spelling of names, places, corporations, or institutions. Even if you are taping the conversation, you should write down all names. The one word a tape recorder can garble better than any other is a name you've never heard before.

Always be listening for the names of other potential sources of information. At the end of your conversation, you may want to ask outright for the names of other persons who might be helpful to you. Again, write this all down, with names, addresses, proper spellings — as much information as your interviewee is willing to give you.

At the end, if it is applicable, also ask for any written material that would help your research. Finally, both as a courtesy and to help you further, ask if you may call to verify information or to ask specific questions about material in the interview.

Follow up on your interview. Write a thank-you note if you can, particularly if the interview was a good one or if you might want to use that source again. If the person inter-viewed will become a major factor in your finished product (whether it's a book, speech, article, report, or paper), you ought to offer to send him or her a copy of your final opus.

However, don't send transcripts of interviews to subjects, even as a courtesy. No one, repeat, no one, ever likes the way they interviewed. Even if you need verification, don't send a transcript but rather excerpt from the section in question or use the telephone. Interviewees will find loads of additional comments, phrasings, and other changes ("I didn't really mean it the way it sounds," or even "I didn't say that" — yes, people will tell you that while knowing that you have it on tape — are common responses to reading a transcript) that will delay your final product, engage you in arguments perhaps, and in all ways transform what was a nicely handled interview-relationship into a "never again" lesson learned. The result of such a contretemps also may be to inhibit your next effort at getting information from people.

5

getting information from libraries

There are over 25,000 libraries in the United States. There are public library systems, branches of public systems, university and college libraries, junior college libraries, libraries within corporations, libraries within museums, libraries in stores, and even libraries in mobile van units. You can safely assume that there is a library near where you live or work. Even Boaz, Alabama, with a population of 5,621 has two libraries (one public; one part of Snead State Junior College) with over 30,000 volumes, films, slides, maps — the works.

Most libraries are free, open five to six days per week, and staffed by professional librarians (persons who went to a graduate school of library science). Most libraries have separate reference rooms staffed by one or more reference librarians. Knowing how to use a library to get information means using these people properly. Although most of us have used libraries to take out books since we were knee-high, we are inherently afraid of those parts of a library that relate to getting information: the card catalog system, the reference room, and the reference librarian. It is time to get rid of the shibboleth that, first, libraries house a vast storehouse of knowledge that only specialists (librarians) can penetrate; and, second, that a librarian will think less of you for not knowing how to use the storehouse without his or her help.

The first step is to familiarize yourself with the overall characteristics of any library you might use regularly. Every library of medium size has printed information describing its hours, collections, specialties and procedures for use. Call your library and ask for one. Or, even better, go in and visit. See where the books are kept. Are they in stacks available to the user or are the stacks tucked away on floors where only librarians and assistants can get at them? What is the procedure for getting a book from the stacks? Must you first consult a card catalogue or printed book catalogues to find the exact title, author, and call number of the book you want? Do you fill out a pre-printed slip of paper, hand it in to someone at a desk, then wait until that person brings you your book; or are you assigned a number, then sent to another room to wait until a number rings on a lit-up board? Is the reference room open (it usually is, even if the main stacks are closed to users) with books accessible on open shelves? Are backdated magazines on open shelves or must you go to a special desk to request these? How do you get at back issues of newspapers? Is there a list of the newspapers and magazines your library keeps or must you consult the card catalogue to find out?

If yours is a large public library, there may be some kinds of material housed in special branches, far away from the main building. In New York, for instance, old newspapers are kept in a warehouse across town from the central research library building, where current issues of newspapers are filed. Still, you needn't go all the way over there to find out *which* newspapers are available, as a copy of the catalogue *is* kept in the central building. You save yourself trips and telephone calls if you first read whatever your library prints about itself. If there is no booklet available, look up your library in the *American Library Directory*.

THE CLASSIFICATION SYSTEM

One of the first facts worth knowing about any library is the system of classification it uses. There's no reason to learn that system in its entirety, but if you have a general understanding of the numbers and/or letters, you'll be able to use the reference room and open stacks on your own without having to depend on a librarian. Particularly in the beginning stages of exploring a subject, it is an advantage to know, generally, where to go in a library.

All libraries classify their material by some system — either Dewey Decimal, Library of Congress, their own, or a combination of these. Major libraries may use one system for a central reference room and another for circulating branches. In New York, the main building (which houses most of the research collections) uses its own classification (which doesn't matter much to the user who can't have access to the stacks anyway), but the open-stack reference branch and all other branches use the Dewey system. (Occasionally, a library will organize specific categories of books differently. Fiction or biography, for instance, might have its own number or letter, though the books will still be arranged within that letter alphabetically by author's or subject's name.) The Library of Congress naturally uses the Library of Congress system, but each card in its catalog gives a corresponding Dewey classification for the book as well. The Dewey system is the oldest, dating from 1895, and most widely used, although many college and university libraries use the Library of Congress system. As a general rule, the larger the library, the more likely it is to use Library of Congress classification. Twenty-one letters allow for more categories of classification than do ten numbers.

Why bother knowing this? Because the way in which your library organizes its books, particularly its reference materials, means you can find books that might provide you with the information you're seeking without having to know a specific title, author, or detailed subject. Put simply, books on religion are shelved near other books on religion; books on Shakespeare (dictionaries, concordances, anything on Shakespeare) are probably near other books on Shakespeare, and they're not merely under "S." You don't want to have to go to a librarian when you're only beginning a research paper on Shakespeare, because you'll ask "Where are your books on Shakespeare?" and he or she will say, "Well, we have lots of books. What exactly are you looking for?" and you don't yet know what exactly you are looking for. If you know this one fact — that in any library that uses the Dewey system, books on Shakespeare are 822.33 and therefore in the 800 shelves — you have given yourself the freedom to explore and thus to begin to structure the right kind of search process.

There is something clean and orderly about the classification systems. They fulfill a rather awesome challenge: The organize all knowledge into categories that are easily knowable, even if the knowledge itself is not. The Dewey system is a number system; the Library of Congress uses letters of the alphabet. (Obviously one way to find out firsthand which your library uses is to look on the spines of books, but as there's always the chance it has its own system, either numbered or lettered, you should ask first.) The Dewey number is always three digits before a decimal point. Whether there are one, two, or more digits *after* the decimal depends on the breadth of the particular library's collection; but there are always three before the decimal. The first digit represents the *class.* Dewey divides all books into ten classes

000	Generalities
100	Philosophy and related disciplines
200	Religion
300	The social sciences
400	Language
500	Pure science
600	Technology (or applied science, like engineering)
700	The arts
800	Literature
900	General geography and history and their auxiliaries

Each class is then further divided into ten *divisions;* the division is connoted by the second digit. The class of Generalities (marked by 0), for instance, contains these ten divisions

010   Bibliographies and catalogs

020   Library and information sciences (You
would find the Library of Congress's own
subject heading here, 025.33.)

030   General encyclopedic works

040   (This is left blank, reserved for one day
when another reference category may
emerge.)

050   General serial publications

060   General organizations and museology (*The
Foundation Directory* can be found here,
061.3.)

070   Journalism, publishing, newspapers (*The
Broadcast News Handbook*, 070.43, in on
this shelf.)

080   General collections

090   Manuscripts and book rarities

Remember, these divisions apply only to the class "Generalities."

Each division, in turn, is made up of ten *sections*, and that completes the Dewey whole number. For the 010 Division, bibliographies and catalogs, the sections are

011   General bibliographies (You'd find books
on reference works here.)

012   Bibliographies of individuals

013   Bibliographies of works by specific classes
of writers

014   Bibliographies of anonymous and
pseudonymous works

015   Bibliographies of works from specific
places (*British Books in Print* is here,
015.42.)

016   Bibliographies of specific disciplines and
subjects (*Government Publications* is here,
016.0157.)

017   General subject catalogs

018   General author and date catalogs (The
       National Union Catalog — the guide to the
       Library of Congress's books, by author — is
       here, 018.1.)

Digits following the decimal indicate further subdivisions; you
do not need to know these unless you're going to be spending a
lot of time (years, perhaps) on one subject. The number 914.5,
for example, (and this can be many shelves or just a few books
on one shelf) has books on the geography of Italy. The three
digits 900, as we have seen, is the class for General Geography
and History. Within that class the division 910 is General
Geography and Travel; within that division is the section 914,
Europe; and the 5 after the decimal is reserved for the country
Italy. Dewey is so orderly a system that its reserved numbers
often apply across the various sections and classes. Italy, for
instance, is connoted by the number 5 after the decimal in the
example above. Books on the history of Italy, though, under
the 940 division (that being the one reserved for History) are
numbered 945, the 5 again being the clue that this number is
kept for Italy. Similarly, books on the Italian language are
under 450, 400 for language and, again, the 5 indicating Italy. I
cite these intricacies merely to point out that you could learn to
use a library without a librarian if you had to.

The Library of Congress Classification System is
letter-based, and all you really need to know is

A   General works — polygraphy
B   Philosophy-religion
C   History — auxiliary science
D   History and topography (except America)
E–F   America
G   Geography and anthropology
H   Social sciences

J	Political science
K	Law
L	Education
M	Music
N	Fine arts
P	Language and Literature
Q	Science
R	Medicine
S	Agriculture — plant and animal industry
T	Technology
U	Military science
V	Naval science
Z	Bibliography and library science

USING A CARD CATALOG

To find a book on a particular subject, the most concrete approach is through the card catalog. The above information is given so that you can actually walk into an open-stack library and find books that have to do with your subject of interest.

The card catalog contains three index cards for each book in the library. Each book has a card filed under the name of its author, its title, and its subject category. The author card gives the most detailed information about the book, its contents, and its location within the library. Several large libraries have printed catalogs (instead of card catalogs) of parts of their collections. You can use books the same way you would the card catalog. They are merely more accessible and easier to transcribe from than the jam-packed index card drawers. In the New York system, all books in the branches are cataloged this way (The catalogs are entitled *Guide to the Branch Libraries.*) Those in the main reference building remain in card catalog files.

The author card can help you determine whether the book is one you should locate. It tells you the book's subject, if its title does not already do so. It tells you how old (and therefore outdated) the work is, whether it has illustrations (you may need pictures), whether it has front matter or a preface (and thus is likely to contain the important acknowledgements and thanks-to-people-sources that might prove valuable. And it gives the height of the book, measured in centimeters. If you will remember that a centimeter is .39 inches (say, one-third of an inch), you will know that a book of unusual height may not be located on the shelf indicated by its call number, but will rather be found shelved spine up (instead of spine out) on a bottom shelf within that section. If the measurements are extraordinarily large, you should ask the librarian where out-sized books are shelved rather than spend the time hunting among books of that number or letter.

When looking up a particular author, you may find hundreds of cards, depending on the size and scope of your

Figure 5-1. From *The Prentice-Hall Handbook for Writers,* 7/E, by Leggett, Mead, and Charvat. Reprinted with permission of Prentice-Hall, Inc. Copyright © 1978 Prentice-Hall, Inc.

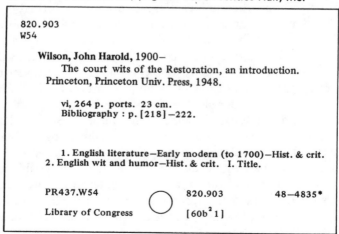

820.903
W54

    Wilson, John Harold, 1900–
        The court wits of the Restoration, an introduction.
    Princeton, Princeton Univ. Press, 1948.

        vi, 264 p. ports. 23 cm.
        Bibliography : p. [218]–222.

        1. English literature—Early modern (to 1700)—Hist. & crit.
    2. English wit and humor—Hist. & crit. I. Title.

    PR437.W54   820.903   48–4835*

    Library of Congress   [60b^{2}1]

library's collection. (Even in a small library, there will probably be one hundred Shakespeare cards, for instance.) The standard order in which the cards will be arranged is: first, cards for collected works of the author; followed by cards for books written by the author, in alphabetical order ("the" is not considered a word in filing); then books edited by the author; then books about the author; and finally, bibliographies of the author's works. This is the usual, but not the only, order. Some libraries classify books of criticism on individual works with the individual works. Others might classify such books with biographies and criticism. If you were looking up Virginia Woolf in the New York Public Library's card catalogue, for example, you'd find 59 cards for works by Virginia Woolf (but these also include books by others on her individual works); followed by ten cards for translations or introductions to others' books; then three bibliographies; then 66 cards for biographies and critical studies of her work. A smaller, general literature library, however, might organize its cards into two categories only: all writings by Virginia Woolf in alphabetical order (including introductions, essays, and even her letters); then all writings on Virginia Woolf, in alphabetical order (and her own diaries are included in this group). As a rule of thumb, then, scan the entire group of cards for an author you are researching; you may find his or her works unusually arranged in your library's card catalog.

Most large libraries do not have open stacks. You fill out a "call slip" for each book you want, then wait for someone to give you your books. Whether you fill out one or not, you should write down the information for any book *you think you want to use* on a separate sheet of paper (index card or notebook, whichever is your system) while you are using the card catalog, that is, while the card is in front of you. You will need to know the call number (in the upper left- or right-hand corner of the card), the author's name (with the right spelling and middle initial), and book title in order to fill out a call slip. But you will do well to include other information on your own

THE NEW YORK PUBLIC LIBRARY ASTOR, LENOX AND TILDEN FOUNDATIONS	Call number:
Author or Periodical:	
Book Title:	
Date/Vol. No.:	
Correct and Legible Name and Address Required	
Name ______	Staff use
Address ______	
City ______ Zip ______	
School or Business ______	form 29d

Figure 5-2. Call slip. Courtesy of The New York Public Library, the Astor, Lenox and Tilden Foundations.

card at this time: dates of author's life; name and place of publisher; publication date; and even subject headings. This card or notation will be part of a working bibliography for whatever project you are researching. If you then find you have used the book in your final product, you will not have to go back and look up all this information again for footnotes and bibliographies.

The card catalog itself tells you how to do research. Look at the last card under any subject or author heading. It may cross-refer you to another related subject heading, one you had not thought of yourself. "See also . . . " in a library's catalog or in any reference work is a valuable tool in taking you one step further into locating information.

THE REFERENCE ROOM
AND THE REFERENCE LIBRARIAN

The library you use may have one general reference room or, if it's a large collection, it may have separate reference rooms for various divisions. (Or, if it's a special library, it will be an entire *reference* library on a particular field.) In any case, there will be at least one general reference room with a librarian in attendance. The room may or may not have its own card catalog of materials.

At the librarian's desk will be several shelves of books. They are the ones most often used to answer ready-reference questions. A dictionary, atlas, almanac, the *U.S. Government Manual, Congressional Directory, Almanac of American Politics* — these are some of the ones you'll find there. If you know that the information you want is likely to be in a general reference book, stop at the desk first, before searching shelves. (However, if this were the only information you needed, you could have obtained it more easily by calling.) The librarian at this desk will probably also have a list of newspapers and magazines kept by that library and the dates for those issues. If you are going to be using periodicals at all, you should keep this list in mind *before* using the *Readers' Guide to Periodical Literature* and writing down every listing under your subject. After all, if your library does not have the periodical, you've wasted a lot of time.

All reference rooms have other materials in common, no matter what their sizes or specialties. There will be a card catalog or printed catalog to guide you to that library's collections. The card catalog will be arranged by author and title and, most likely, by subject also. (Some very small libraries advise you not to trust their subject headings but to search via author and title if you know them.) If there is a printed catalogue — which means you are in a large library — it will probably have separate volumes for "Authors" (or "Names"), "Titles," and "Subjects," and each of these will be further

divided into alphabetical volumes. There will be the *Readers'*
Guide to Periodical Literature, at least one multivolume set of
encyclopedias, the *New York Times Index,* and other standard
reference works. There will be directories, catalogs, bibliographies, anything that would fit under the 000 Generalities class,
as explained earlier in this chapter. (See Chapter Six for an
analysis of the specific reference materials you find in libraries.)

Your reference room may have its periodicals on
open shelves, that is, bound volumes of *Time, Newsweek, Scientific American,* and whatever else it keeps, going back to first
issues; or these may be filed in an out-of-the-way location where
a library assistant gets you the issue you want. The standard
reference room also has at least one photocopying machine and
one microfilm reader machine if only to use for reading back
issues of the *New York Times* and your local newspaper. It may
have other microform (cards) readers and audio-visual equipment, again depending on size and scope; it may or may not
have government materials, depending on whether it serves as an
official government deposit library. Even if it doesn't, though,
your library probably has a vertical file of some kind. These are
loose materials — booklets, pamphlets, study reports, perhaps
even dissertations on specific subjects — filed on their own,
away from the periodicals or reference books. Always ask a
librarian for a description of what the vertical files contain and
how you go about using them. The next chapter will help you
know how and when to use the materials in your reference
room. For now, just know what general types are there.

The most important resource in the reference room
is the librarian. He or she can be a useful tool or an obstacle to
your search for information. You will become the major
determinant of how helpful that person will be. Today's librarian is an educated, trained, and highly informed specialist. He or
she knows what reference material is *out there* (or in there, in
the library) and how it is to be used. But the librarian also has a
heavy volume of materials and users to deal with, and little time
to do it in.

In an ideal situation, you and the librarian would

hold a reference interview, even if your question were a short and specific one. The librarian would try to figure out what information you are asking for, how that information relates to the system of that particular library, and how much information you actually want. A really good librarian would also determine how deeply and at what level of complexity you wish to explore your subject, and would find this out by ascertaining your purpose for doing the research. Then the librarian would guide you in the use of the materials.

That probably won't happen. A more likely scenario is one in which the user doesn't know the language of the system and feels ignorant confronting the librarian. As a result the user winds up either not asking at all or asking for help in terms so general that the librarian is unable to help without spending a lot of time figuring out what is being asked.

You must do your own translating to libraries; that means you must put your question for information in terms that the librarian can understand and act on. He or she represents an information system that has been codified along certain lines (bibliographies, directories, et al.). You, the user, come in with an entirely different lexicon; your question may not contain one word that relates to the library's language.

How do you get around that problem? First, you "key-word" your informational need. Key-wording and associating are helpful ways of organizing any information hunt. (You'll see later how they can get you started on large research projects.) If your question, for example, is "I have to find out if there's a bill anywhere under consideration that would regulate advertising rates charged by television stations and what the effects of that might be," you have already given key-words: the librarian will hear "advertising rates/television networks/ legislation" (implies "federal" since it's nationally controlled) and will be able to relate those terms to specific reference works in the collection. But if you say "I need information on government scientific experiments" when what you want is material on the use of animals in federal medical product-testing, you haven't done the proper translation.

As a rule, be as specific as you can. If you want information on bicycles because you are planning to buy one and want to know which kind to buy, then say so. Don't ask for "a book on biking" or "something on modern bicycles." Librarians say the greatest problem they encounter in dealing with you, the user, is that the questions put to them are too vague — that when what you want to know is "Who in this country sells artist so-and-so's work?" you come in and ask "What do you have on contemporary artists?" He or she must then narrow you down through the gamut of "Are you looking for pictures of works? or criticism? or any specific school of painting? or biographical information? or perhaps a particular kind of art? and so on. You could have made it a lot simpler for yourself if you had merely asked your question right the first time. And don't worry that the librarian has never heard of the particular artist. Then the ball is in his or her court; the librarian will have to ask "Is that artist a painter or sculptor? an American or European? dead or alive?" and all the other questions that key into that library's reference materials. Librarians can cope with the question that's too precise; it's the general ones that they'll shun.

If you have already explored other routes to the information you seek, tell the librarian that fact when you ask your question. You have to let him or her know where you are in the information searching process and how much further you're willing to go. The following is an example of what can happen: While reading a biography I came across a mention of an early twentieth-century English writer who had become an expert, on the side, on Egyptian pottery. Knowing someone who is beginning to collect books on pottery, I thought this writer's work might be of interest. I guessed that the books would be out of print by now, but might still be obtained from a book search service or old bookshop if one knew the titles, publisher, and dates. The writer in question was not a well-known name, either then or now, and his reputation today is based on his works of literary, not art, criticism.

I went to a small library (private) nearby, whose

specialty is general literature from England and America, nineteenth and twentieth centuries. The general biographical dictionaries there (*Dictionary of National Biography*, for instance, which profiles the lives of British well-knowns) either didn't list this writer at all, or had a listing so scanty that it didn't include mention of his complete works. I told the reference librarian I had checked those volumes and couldn't find anything. He matter-of-factly sent me to another biographical dictionary, one I had not looked in. Finding nothing there, I returned to his desk, and this time he pulled a volume from his shelf which turned out to be a bibliography of nineteenth- and twentieth-century books on art, a book whose existence I was not aware of. But it wasn't there, either. And at this point he looked me over, then said, "Let's go upstairs." We went to a small private office on the top floor of this library's building and on glass-enclosed shelves there were what seemed an endless number of volumes entitled, *General Catalogue of Printed Books* (London: Trustees of the British Museum, 1959–1966). The information was there. I never would have thought of that exact source — I didn't know it was in this particular library — and was more than a little disappointed that I had had to spend time "proving" my interest in finding the information before the librarian really helped me.

Another guideline to follow in unlocking librarians is the same one mentioned in discussing interviews. Question the answer you get. If the librarian says, "What you want is *Ulrich's*" and you don't know what exactly that is, ask now. "What is it? What does it contain? Where is it? How do I use it? Is it by date, or alphabetical by subject, or by name?" You're not supposed to have been born knowing these things, after all. Make the librarian give you the information you need, even if it's information about a source you're going to consult for the information you need. At the very least, you'll come out of the library having found out about a new source of information and how to use it. And it will stay in the back of your mind that this source exists, that there's a book called *Ulrich's*, which lists foreign magazine articles by subject.

Sometimes you must be creative, even in front of the librarian. If you are learning to be a good searcher, you imagine the perfect source to exist, then figure out how to locate it. By using that process, you can give the librarian ideas that might not otherwise have occurred to him or her. "If there were a book that listed all manufacturers of X-ray equipment in the U.S." may seem like a silly way to query a librarian, but there may very well be such a book, or one similar, and your first question might not have triggered recall of that source in the librarian's mind. Make up the perfect source; then let the librarian tell you it doesn't exist.

In some situations, you may be able to ask a librarian to give more extensive help. Many large public library systems have Readers' Advisory Services, which, although they will not do scholarly research for you, may still work up a list of books for you to consult on a specific subject. In smaller libraries, you may find persons who have more time and who think of themselves as detectives. Your local librarian may get interested enough in your search to do a lot more than guide you to one or two reference sources. And in the special libraries, as we shall see, you can find a wide range of research possibilities, from the research-for-a-fee service to the librarian who is paid to get you the information you need for your job. Keep in mind that somewhere there is a librarian who will spend the time, expertise, and inclination in order to assist you. When I have needed such help quickly and the telephone lines are busy in New York libraries, I have fallen back on my old college library. You might think of additional out-of-the-way libraries that you could rely on in an "emergency."

THE LIBRARY OF CONGRESS: HOW TO USE IT FROM AFAR

This is the most special library in the United States, and yet very few people outside Washington ever use its services. As I said in Chapter Two, you should make sure you have a copy of its publications, *Information for Readers* and *Services to the Nation,* both of which you can get, free, by writing: Library of Congress, Central Services Division, Washington, D.C., 20540. Once you know about this place, you will use it frequently.

The Library of Congress is the largest library in the world, and it is primarily a reference library. Under ordinary circumstances you may not take books out of it. Its chief purpose is to provide Congress with whatever information that body needs to do its job. The Library's major unit for administering this function is the Congressional Research Service. Strictly speaking, the five hundred researchers there work only for Congress. They answer small fact-finding inquiries, do the legwork on lists of questions and carry on in-depth studies on any subject as well. Sometimes these are made at the specific request of a congressperson or committee, but just as often, they're done in anticipation of future congressional needs. Many of these reports, called *Congressional Research Reports,* are published and compiled in an annual index. These studies are factually presented arguments for and against various courses of action; they include historical background, synopses, bibliographic information — in short, everything you'd need to know about a current subject from natural gas deregulation to the fate of the sperm whale. The service also produces *Bill Digests,* which give the content, history, sponsors' names, and course of action taken on all bills before the current session; another information source, *Current Issue Briefs,* are computerized condensations of issues before Congress. There is a printed listing of these briefs.

These services and publications are prepared for Congress, not for you. But Congress works for you, and therein lies your access to this material. If you think you might one day have a need for any of these studies, or even if you're simply curious and want to see what's available in your field, call your congressperson's office now. Ask an aide there to call the Congressional Research Service in the Library of Congress (he or she may not know of it) and request the annual index of the *Reports* and the listing of the *Briefs.* The aide should mail those to you when they come in. Then, whenever you want a particular report or brief, use your congressperson's office once again, this time requesting the specific item.

The other divisions of the Library are *directly* open to you, either in person or by mail or telephone. At the library itself are sixteen separate reading rooms, each with its own reference collection and librarian staff. In addition, there is the General Reference and Bibliography Division, which can, by telephone or mail, field your inquiries to the right reference division. The general reference room will suggest bibliographies (in response to written requests), but not with scholarly depth. For that, you must contact the appropriate reference librarian.

The Library's Prints and Photograph Division contains over eight million pictures, drawing, posters, negatives and even motion pictures, all on some aspect of American history and life. If you show up in person, the division will help you locate ones you might need; or it can recommend picture researchers who will do the legwork for you, for a fee. You can have the pictures you want photoduplicated there and mailed to you. Ask for a list of fees and the appropriate forms from the Photoduplicating Service. They will apply to any other reference materials you might want duplicated and sent.

In Chapter Three I mentioned the Library's National Referral Center as a good place to go with a specific question. That division will give you the names of organizations that can act as "experts" for you. Chapter Six will cover the Library's computerized information sources. For now, you should know that the Library of Congress *does* have data bases and through them, can quickly get at the bibliographic, legislative (bill digest), and expert referral information described here. In response to a written request from you, the General Reference and Bibliography Division may indeed use the computer to give you your answers. For more extensive data base searches, you may have to pay a fee.

Another specific research arm of the Library of Congress is its Science and Technology Division, which is a good place to query if (1) the subject you're researching falls within the sciences; and (2) your own library is either too small or is

LC Science Tracer Bullet

Reference Section, Science and Technology Division
Library of Congress, 10 First Street, S.E., Washington, D.C. 20540

ISSN 0090-5232

WOMEN IN THE SCIENCES
Compiled by Constance Carter

TB 76-2 March 1976

SCOPE: A guide to sources chronicling the history and contributions of women in the field of science.

Introductions to the topic appear in:

Lonsdale, Kathleen. Women in science: reminiscences and reflections. Impact of science on society, v. 20, no. 1, Jan./Mar. 1970: 45-59. Q1.I4 and Vertical file*

Zuckerman, Harriet, and Jonathan R. Cole. Women in American science. Minerva, v. 13, no. 1, spring 1975: 82-102. AS121.M5

SUBJECT HEADINGS under which books on women in the sciences can be located in the LC card and book catalogs and the on-line computer terminal in the Science Reading Room include the following:

WOMEN SCIENTISTS
WOMEN ENGINEERS
WOMEN PHYSICIANS
WOMEN IN MEDICINE
WOMEN IN AERONAUTICS
WOMEN MATHEMATICIANS
WOMEN PHYSICISTS
WOMEN--BIBLIOGRAPHY

BASIC TEXTS

Mead, Kate Campbell Hurd. A history of women in medicine, from the earliest times to the beginning of the nineteenth century. Boston, Milford House, 1973. 569 p. R692.M38 1973
Reprint of the 1938 ed. published by Haddam Press, Haddam, Conn.

* Available in the reference collection, Science Reading Room
**Available in the microform collection, Science Reading Room

Figure 5-3. From *LC Science Tracer Bullet* 76-2, March 1976. Reprinted with permission of the Library of Congress.

weak in current scientific and technical resources. The Division will help you locate a book, pamphlet, technical report, or dissertation by searching its own collection (probably through its data base systems). In addition, the reference section of this division publishes a series of guides, called *Tracer Bullets,* which provide bibliographies for particular scientific subjects. These are invaluable research tools (if they include your subject, that is): the bibliographies are broken down into introductory materials; subject headings under which to look in the library; basic texts; related texts; general works that include your subject; journal articles and conference proceedings; and lists of more detailed bibliographies on your topic. They are not only useful bibliographies, but also suggest key-words and subject headings that you might have overlooked. Write to the Reference Section, and ask for a current list of already published *Tracer Bullets;* then order the ones you want. There is no charge. Examples of recent *Tracer Bullet* subjects are: Alcohol Fuels; Sports Medicine; Brain and Behavior; Energy Resources in China; Microwaves; and Cosmology. If your occupation or outside interests touch on any scientific areas — pure or applied sciences — you ought to have these bibliographic guides on hand, as part of your own reference collection.

SPECIAL LIBRARIES

In addition to the Library of Congress, your own public library system, and the libraries in nearby colleges and universities, there are thousands of libraries whose collections center around one or two specialty fields. You'll find these libraries within large corporations (perhaps your own), small clubs, museums, churches, in buildings you've passed but never looked in, with names you've never heard before.

Special libraries are in many ways more valuable to the information seeker than the larger, extensive public library systems. If their areas of specialty coincide with the subject of your search, then their collections may go much deeper than those in your public library. Yet because they are smaller, the special libraries are easier to use. You find that the book you're looking for is actually on the shelf (instead of missing or not-yet-shelved or taken out, which is often the case in large public libraries), and you can locate it without having to fill out call slips or go through library assistants. You also will be able to figure out the classification system of a smaller, specialty library by merely looking around; or there will be a piece of paper somewhere listing its method of shelving. There won't be lines for the microfilm readers, the reference books are apt to be out on open shelves instead of behind a librarian's desk, and I suspect you'll find it a more comfortable place in which to work.

Some of the special libraries are public-private, you may use their reference services for free but must be a paying member to take out books; others are entirely private but will, upon application, open their research facilities to you. *The American Library Directory* lists most of these, by state and by town alphabetically within each state. Each listing gives information about a particular library's hours, subject interests, special collections, size and breadth of materials, and qualifications for use. Your library will probably have a copy of this directory. The only drawback to this volume is that the libraries are listed only alphabetically, although there are letters by each listing to indicate whether the library is a college, medical, law, religious or "special" unit. That means that if you are looking for a library that specializes in naval history, for instance, and you live in a large city, you must read through a number of listings before finding the right library. In New York, there are hundreds of libraries keyed as "special," but you must comb through the entries to find, say, which ones are art libraries. What you find, however, is a wide range, from the Frick Art Reference Library to the Butterick Patterns Archives/Library, the Goethe Institute (specialty: German art), and the Laboratory Institute of Merchandising Library. If your field of work or interests includes the arts, it would be worthwhile to read through the listings for New York or the largest city near you, and extract the libraries that specify that emphasis in their collections.

Another reference book on libraries is the *Directory of Special Libraries and Information Centers*, 5th ed. (Detroit: Gale Research Company, 1979). This work lists libraries within the United States and Canada alphabetically, but has a subject index as well. The listings are also more detailed, written in ordinary English (as opposed to librarian language) and include specific information about automated information retrieval systems.

Make up your own index of libraries (on cards or in files) if you want to have the listings for your city at arm's

Figure 5-4. From the *Directory of Special Libraries and Information Centers,* 5th edition. Reprinted with permission of Gale Research Company. Copyright © 1979 Gale Research Company.

★8926★
SAN FERNANDO VALLEY COLLEGE OF LAW - LIBRARY (Law)
8353 Sepulveda Blvd.   Phone: (213) 894-5711
Sepulveda, CA 91343   James G. Sherman, Lib.Dir.
Founded: 1962. **Staff:** Prof 4; Other 1. **Subjects:** Law. **Holdings:** 40,000 books and bound periodical volumes; 22,000 microforms (cataloged). **Subscriptions:** 203 journals and other serials. **Services:** Library open to public. **Formerly:** University of San Fernando Valley - College of Law.

★8927★
SAN FRANCISCO ACADEMY OF COMIC ART - LIBRARY (Art; Hum)
2850 Ulloa   Phone: (415) 681-1737
San Francisco, CA 94116   Bill Blackbeard, Dir.
Founded: 1968. **Staff:** 5. **Subjects:** Science fiction; crime fiction; popular literature; comic strip art in all aspects; dime novels; pulp and other popular magazines; motion picture data; critical literature. **Special Collections:** Sherlockiana; Oz books; foreign popular literature; children's books; nationally representative bound newspaper runs, including many rare Hearst papers. **Holdings:** 50,000 books; one million comic strips (cataloged); 22,000 unbound periodicals; manuscripts; original comic strips and other graphic work; movie stills and pressbooks; newspaper and magazine ads and art; science fiction fanzines and fanzines of other areas of interest; century-long complete bound newspaper files; segregated editorial pages, columns, film and auto sections, comic strips. **Subscriptions:** 100 journals and other serials; 100 newspapers. **Services:** Interlibrary loans; copying; library open to public by appointment. **Staff:** Dean Dickensheet, Dir.; Shirley Dickensheet, Dir.; Anne Lecture, Dir.; Gale Paulson, Dir.

length. Mine, for New York, uses the following categories: Art; Business, Economics and Finance; College and University; Communications Media; General Literature; Government and Politics; Insurance (there are seven large ones in New York, open to the public); International Affairs; Labor; Law; Medicine; Religion; Rights; and Miscellaneous (which, on my list, includes the American Kennel Club Library, the Cigar Association of America Library and the M. N. and C. V. Young Library of Mnemonics). I also keep a separate list of picture libraries, again specifying their scope and subject specialties.

The best way to use special libraries is by telephone. If you're considering a visit, first call to verify what the *Directory* said about the library: its hours and availability to the public. Query the librarian on the telephone the same way you would approach a librarian in person. Be specific: "I am doing research on Carl Jung" or "I am trying to show the application of Jung's dream theories to modern-day therapy situations. Would you have any materials I could use?" That detailed information-giving approach will not only save you a wasted trip but may get you into a library that is otherwise not open to the public. Many special libraries, particularly those within private corporations, will let "serious researchers" use their materials. The more "special" a library is, the more you are likely to find a librarian who can help you get information. If your field is his or her field, you have, after all, found an *expert*. Don't be afraid to ask that librarian all the questions you have about where to look. The worst that can happen is that he or she will hang up; the best is that you've tapped into a valuable research resource that you can draw on again and again.

6

reference works

At one point in the information-getting process you simply want to know what book to go to. The assumption is that a reference book exists for any subject you wish to find out about. That assumption is nearly valid.

Chapters Two and Three cited specific titles to keep on your arms' length bookshelf, plus the two essentials, *Encylopedia of Associations* and the *Research Centers Directory*, which you may either buy yourself or use at the library. Chapter Seven will cover government information as a "kind" of reference material deserving extensive exploration on its own. Additionally, the Appendix lists, by subject, those works that will be helpful to persons in varying fields or avocations (public relations, finance, design, and so on).

That still leaves a vast collection of materials that one ought to know about, some of them by name. There are full-length books that are lists of reference books, but yet barely skim the surface of what is out there. No one work can list them all (but see the Appendix for a selected list of these). Better than knowing the names of all of them, however, is a familiarity with the *kinds* of works that exist, the best or most used examples of each kind, and guidelines on how to use them. The kinds of materials you should know about are: bibliographies; biographical works; periodicals; newspapers; indexes and abstracts to books, periodicals, newspapers, and reports; microforms; pictures; and data bases. Of course, there are other kinds of reference books — dictionaries, atlases, and handbooks on various subjects — but these seem to me to be sources with which most people are familiar, if not with exact titles, at least with how to use them. Also, many of these are mentioned in other chapters or in the Appendix listing.

A bibliography is a list of reference materials. It may be a list of books on a particular subject; it may be a list of books and magazines in a particular language; it may be a list of films or newspapers; is may be a long list or a short "selected" one. The major reference tool you have for finding out about a subject is your library's card catalog. And *that* is a bibliography itself. But that is not always the best definition of *what is out there* in the form of reference materials on your subject.

By far the largest definition in the United States of what published information is out there is provided by the Library of Congress's *The National Union Catalog: A Cumulative Author List,* 1956 to date (Washington, D.C.: Library of Congress, 1958 to date); and its companion source, *The National Union Catalog: Pre–1956 Imprints* (London: Mansell, 1968 to date). The first shows the holdings of more than 750 major libraries in the United States, and lists by author (or main entry, where author is not known) each work published since 1956 that is in the Library of Congress. The second gives the complete card holdings of the Library from 1901 to 1956 — there will be 610 volumes when completed — again, by author and main entry. "Work" is not merely books, but magazines, maps, and all other forms of printed material, though for some of the other forms there are more complete bibliographies than the *NUC.* Doctoral dissertations, for example, are recorded more thoroughly in *Dissertation Abstracts International,* although if a dissertation has been sent in to the Library of Congress or reported on a card by one of its *NUC* member libraries, it will appear in the *Catalog.* Similarly, there are better listings of periodicals, though the *Catalog* certainly includes them, too.

The *Catalog* is a monthly, with quarterly, annual, five- and ten-year cumulations. Each entry is actually a photographed card, like the one that you'd find in your library's

NM 021014   MH CLU PPL ICN ICU IU

Marriott, Thomas, d. 1766, supposed author.
    Sentimental fables
        see under [Marryat, Thomas] 1730-
1792.

Marriott, Thomas, d. 1766.
    The twentieth epistle of Horace
        see under Horatius Flaccus, Quintus.
[Supplement]

Marriott, Thomas Lechmere.
    Gas consumer's manual: containing the Gas
measurement act of 1859, with a full index
and observations on the passage of the
bill through Parliament, and a practi-

NM 0241021   00

Marriott, Victor Edward, 1882–   ,ed.
    Kagawa and cooperatives, edited by Victor Edward
Marriott. Chicago, Ill.: The Kingdom of God fellow-
ship, 1936.   15 p.   21 cm.

    1. Co-operation.   2. Kagawa,   Toyahiko, 1888–
N.Y.P.L.,   January 25, 1938

NM 0241022   NN OrP DNAL MH

Zeta   Marriott, W
Mgp69   The Italian Swiss Protestants of the Grisons.
M34   By Dr. Marriott ... With two introductory
              prefaces by . . . Baptist W. Noel . . . and . . .
            James Currie . . . London, Partridge and Oakey,
              Continental Protestant depot [1846]
              viii, 39, [1] p.   14 cm.
              Reprinted from the "Continental echo."

NM 0241023   CtY

Figure 6-1.   Reprinted by permission of MIPL and the American Library Association from *National Union Catalog Pre-1956 Imprints*, copyright © 1974 by Mansell Information Publishing Limited and the American Library Association.

card catalog; it gives author's name and dates, subject headings and description of contents — the same as a typical author card in your library. But the *Catalog* also notes which libraries have copies of each book listed. It you need a title that is not in your library's collection, ask a librarian to verify the title through the *Catalog,* then see if you can obtain it through an interlibrary loan. If that is not possible, you can then make arrangements to have the owning library photocopy sections of the work you require for your research.

If you live in a large city, your public library system is a *NUC* member library and there is probably a *NUC* telephone number which you can call to find out which branch in your system has the work you're looking for.

These two author catalogs can help you verify information about a particular author and specific works. (If the dates, or spellings, or contents description should differ from information on your library's card catalog, it's your library that's incorrect.) They also help you locate works your library does not own. For them to be of help, however, you must have an author's name.

If you need to find out what books exist in a particular subject area, the road into the *NUC* is through U.S. Library of Congress Catalogs, *Subject Catalog, 1950 to date* (Washington, D.C.: Library of Congress, 1955 to date). These volumes cross-reference every entry in the *NUC,* by subject, but only for material published after 1945 (the subtitle says "1950" but the cards go back before that date). The *Subject Catalog* is issued quarterly with annual and five-year cumulations.

The other best bibliography on "everything ever published" is the British Museum's *General Catalogue of Printed Books* (London: Trustees of the British Museum, 1959–1966), its various supplements (five- and ten-year supplements bring it constantly up to date) and the companion *Subject Index,* which covers works added since 1880. The *General Catalogue* contains all printed books in the Museum from the fifteenth century up to 1955, and the supplements continue the holdings from that date on. There are over six million entries in the 263-volume main catalog. Only in the last two centuries will you find any duplication between this bibliography and the Library of Congress's *Catalogs*. For that reason, many smaller libraries, (usually nonpublic ones) that have to choose between one set or the other opt for the British Museum's catalog as the all-inclusive source. You should inquire, then scan whichever of these your library owns.

The works mentioned above are the giants of the bibliographic lot. They verify and locate material that exists in print in the world. However, when you want books on a subject but have no author or title to go by, a more helpful work is *The United States Catalog* 4th Ed. (New York: Wilson, 1928) and its modern extension, the *Cumulative Book Index, 1928 to date* (CBI) (New York: Wilson, 1933 to date). Compiled annually since 1898, the two list most books published in English by author, title, and subject. The subject headings are numerous and easy to use. CBI comes out monthly, then is bound into an annual volume. Most libraries will have it or its chief competitor, the *American Book Publishing Record* (ABPR) (New York: Bowker, Sept. 1974 to date). Both works record English-language books at the time of publication. If you wish to find a book that is currently in print, whether it was originally published last year or thirty years ago, the source to consult is *Books in Print* (New York: Bowker, 1948 to date), which goes back to 1948. *Books in Print* is published annually in December and is then supplemented in the following Spring. It and a companion *Subject Guide to Books in Print* are more frequently used to obtain information about books than any other source. Each entry shows title and author, price, name of publisher and the forms and editions in which a book is currently in print. The *Subject Guide* also lists addresses for U.S. and Canadian publishers. Most libraries and bookstores, no matter how small, will have copies of *Books In Print,* the *Subject Guide,* and its other companion works: *Paperbound Books in Print, Children's Books in Print,* and *Subject Guide to Children's Books in Print.* Knowing that bookstores have these should save you time in verifying the existence of a work

SPORTS
see also Amusements; Athletics; Games; Gymnastics; Olympic Games; Outdoor Life; Photography of Sports; Physical Education and Training; Rodeos; Track-Athletics; Winter Sports also names of sports, e.g. Golf

Atkinson, George & Bengtsson, Hans. Orienteering for Sport & Challenge. LC 75-41872. (Environmental Sports Ser). 1976. 8.95 (ISBN 0-8289-0271-2); pap. 4.95x (ISBN 0-8289-0270-4). Greene.

Consumer Guide Magazine, ed. Spectators Guide to Sports: Rules, Scoring, Strategy & Competing. 1976. pap. 5.95 (G9975, Sig). NAL.

Cozens, Frederick W. & Stumpf, Florence S. Sports in American Life. LC 75-22810. (America in Two Centuries Ser). 1976. Repr. of 1953 ed. 21.00x (ISBN 0-405-07681-9). Arno.

Diagram Group. Rules of the Game. large-format ed. 1976. pap. 6.95 (ISBN 0-553-01015-8, M1015). Bantam.

Koppett, Leonard. Game Plans & Super Scouts. 1976. 8.95; pap. 4.95. G&D.

McWhirter, Norris & McWhirter, Ross. Guinness Sports Record Book, 1976-77. (Illus.). 1976. 4.95 (ISBN 0-8069-0030-X); lib. bdg. 4.89 (ISBN 0-8069-0031-8). Sterling.

Marsh, Irving T., et al, eds. Best Sports Stories 1976: A Panorama of the 1975 Sports World, with the Year's Top Photographs. (Illus.). 1976. 8.95 (ISBN 0-525-06622-5). Dutton.

Novak, Michael. The Joy of Sports. 1976. 10.00. Basic.

Offical Rules of Sports & Games. 1976. text ed. 22.50x (ISBN 0-392-05512-0, SpS). Soccer.

Reichler, Joe. The Game & the Glory. 1976. 19.95 (ISBN 0-13-346072-X). P-H.

Yee, Min S. & Wright, Donald K. The Sports Book. 1976. pap. 6.95 (ISBN 0-553-01017-4, M1017). Bantam.

Figure 6-2. From *Subject Guide to Books in Print, 1975-1976.* Reprinted with permission of R. R. Bowker Company. Copyright © 1976 by Xerox Corporation.

in print and the specific information about its author, title, and publisher.

I have cited here only bibliographies in English. There are as well all-inclusive lists of books published in foreign countries and in foreign languages. Some are current (like *Books in Print*), while others are retrospective records of "everything ever published."

That brings one to more narrowly selected bibliographic lists of works, books (or materials) within a field or on a specific subject – say, the *Bibliography of Bioethics* or *Literature of the Film.* Thousands exist. Check the Appendix of this book, your library's reference shelves (remembering the Dewey system, you know they will be the first shelves in the reference section), and the catalogues of the major reference book publishers, Bowker, Gale, and Wilson. Additionally, there are several good guides to reference books, which list titles. By necessity, most are selective, not complete. But these may provide you with a general picture of the field of reference works.

The very best is William A. Katz's *Introduction to Reference Work,* Volume I: Basic Information Sources (New York: McGraw-Hill Book Company, 1978). Though written for librarians, it is a most thorough and readable run-through of specific sources — books, bibliographies, services, the works. Your library will have a copy.

A valuable paperback guide, which you should obtain for your bookshelf, is Marion V. Bell and Eleanor A. Swidan's *Reference Books: A Brief Guide,* 8th ed. (Baltimore: Enoch Pratt Free Library, 1978). This small and handy book lists selective reference titles first by type of work (bibliographic, encyclopedic, etc.), then by subject field. It is by no means complete, but the descriptions of materials are clear and its size means you can bring it along with you to the library when researching a subject. You can obtain a copy from the Enoch Pratt Library for $2.50. See the Appendix for others.

If knowing what's out there to you means seeing the books about the books about the books, you will want to look at *The Bibliographic Index:* A Cumulative Bibliography of Bibliographies (New York: Wilson, 1938 to date) or Theodore Besterman's *World Bibliography of Bibliographies,* 4th ed. (Lausanne: Societas Bibliographica, 1965–66). The first is published three times a year, lists bibliographies about subjects, persons, and places. You look up your subject and note all the bibliographies listed. Then you must locate and consult each of those bibliographies, noting each book listed in each; then finally, you must find the books themselves. Besterman's book is similar, although there are only 16,000 subject headings, and the lists end with 1965. As large as they are, neither work is all-inclusive. Many bibliographies that are in periodicals are not included (there are simply too many periodicals) and new bibliographies are published continuously, which somewhat dates these works. Still, if you are an expert (or wish to become one) bent on exploring as much material as you can find on your subject, you may find these lists essential.

You will be relieved (or perhaps disappointed) to know that there is no one bibliography of everything ever published everywhere.

BIOGRAPHICAL WORKS

As you've seen, biographical reference works are valuable if you're trying to locate someone well-known or prepare for an interview with that person; they're helpful also if you're trying to find a list of an author's works or even if you merely want to "place" someone in the right time and field.

Biographical dictionaries and indexes may be divided into two basic types: those that contain profiles of deceased persons and those that include living subjects. But there are many further subdivisions and specialties within the genre: biographies by country (*Who's Who in America,* for example); and other unique lines of demarcation (*American Catholic Who's Who*).

The standard one-volume biographical reference source is *Webster's Biographical Dictionary* (Springfield, Mass.: G. & C. Merriam Company, 1972), a Who's Who-type dictionary that lists 40,000 individuals, mostly well-known deceased Americans and English subjects. It is a good first stop when seeking information about a well-known person. The entries are short, befitting a dictionary format.

Called a dictionary as well, but really more on the order of an encyclopedia is the *Dictionary of American Biography* (New York: Charles Scribner's Sons, 1928–1944), a 20-volume work with separate index and five-year supplements covering the years up to 1955. The DAB is the most well-known

American biographical dictionary and contains over 16,000 articles on deceased individuals who have made significant contributions to American life (some foreigners are included under this heading).

The DAB is modelled after *the* English-language biographical work, *The Dictionary of National Biography* (London: Oxford University Press, 1922) with seven ten-year *Supplements* that cover the years up to 1970. Containing twice as many entries as the American DAB, this work is the best source to begin with when looking up deceased British (including the colonies) subjects in any walk of life. The entries are thorough, lucid, signed articles with useful bibliographies given at the end. Originally edited by Leslie Stephen (father of Virginia Woolf) and Sidney Lee, the present 63-volume work has over 32,000 biographies.

Three very useful biographical indexes to material appearing in journals, magazines, and books are *Biography Index* (New York: Wilson, January 1946 to date); *Biographical Dictionaries Master Index 1975-1976* (Detroit: Gale, 1965); and *The New York Times Obituaries Index 1858-1968* (New York: The New York Times, 1970). The first of these is a quarterly publication that indexes material in biographical books and over two thousand periodicals. Each issue contains an index by profession and occupation. The *Master Index* is an index to over 80,000 biographies (mostly living Americans) collected from *Who's Who* and other biographical dictionaries. The *Times'* obituary index directs you to the page and column of that newspaper on which an individual's obituary appeared. All three are good vehicles for locating background material about persons whose names you know.

As you might have guessed, there are books *on* biographical books and indexes. A thorough scan of this field is made by Robert B. Slocum's *Biographical Dictionaries and Related Works* (Detroit: Gale, 1967) and its *Supplement* (1972), which lists over 8,000 titles, indexed by subject, title, and author.

Strictly speaking, a periodical means any publication issued periodically, which would include newspapers. But as these merit their own analysis as research resources, I'll use periodicals here to mean magazines and journals. Another word you'll see used in your library may be "serials," which encompasses both magazines (and journals) and newspapers in its meaning. If a reference book you're consulting says "serials" it should include both; it it says only "periodicals," it will probably refer you only to magazines.

The *Union List of Serials in Libraries of the United States and Canada,* edited by Edna Brown Titus, 3rd ed. (New York: Wilson, 1965) and its updated volumes do for periodicals what the *National Union Catalog* does for books. You will not need it for most search projects, but it is worth knowing about if you ever must verify and/or locate a specialized periodical that your library won't have. You can then contact the library that has the work and ask the reference librarian to consult *Serials* for you and have him or her photocopy the article or sections for you.

The directories and guides to periodicals that you will want to use yourself are these: *Ulrich's International Periodicals Directory,* 16th ed., 1975-1976 (New York: Bowker, 1975). This is a most valuable list of periodicals, both foreign and domestic. Under 250 subject headings, alphabetically arranged, entries show date, frequency, price, editor, location, and other particulars for over 60,000 periodicals. You would use *Ulrich's* to find out which periodicals exist within your subject area. Looking up "Business and Economics Investments," for instance, you'd find a list of fully described journals and magazines, ranging from the *Perth Stock Exchange Official Record* to *Standard & Poor's Bond Guide. Ulrich's* will not help you locate an actual article about your subject. Like the *National Union Catalog,* it is a bibliographic directory rather than a guide to the contents of periodicals.

Readers' Guide to Periodical Literature (New York: Wilson, 1905 to date) is the work you'll use most often to start off a search. Practically every library in the United States receives the ubiquitous green volumes. The guide indexes articles appearing in 160 general-interest American magazines since 1900. Paperback volumes arrive at your library semi-monthly from September to June, monthly for July and August. These are then put into a cumulative one-year index and later into thicker (still green) volumes that cover several years' worth of articles. Approaching the *Readers' Guide* to find out about a subject, you would begin with the most recent volumes (paper), looking up your subject in each one. If your subject is actually an author he or she will be in the general index listed alphabetically as a subject. You note the volume, date, and page number of the article you'll want to read, then find the appropriate volume of that magazine (if your library keeps these on open shelves) or fill out a call slip with that information on it. Before you go to the trouble of noting article information, however, you should ask to see the list of periodicals kept by

Figure 6-3. From *Readers' Guide to Periodical Literature.* Copyright © 1980 by The H. W. Wilson Company. Material reproduced by permission of the publishers.

ILLINOIS Institute of Technology, Chicago
   With a dose of morality; professional ethics courses, D. Milesko-Pytel. il Am Educ 15:31-6 Ja '79
ILLINOIS State University, Normal
   From traditional to competency-based teacher education and back again: an eight-year experiment. M. A. Lorber. Phi Delta Kappan 60:523-4 Mr '79; Discussion. bibl 61:194-5 N '79
ILLITERACY
   Common enemy; illiteracy. C. Friedland. Pub W 215:107 F 26 '79
   Cult of ignorance. I. Asimov. por Newsweek 95:19 Ja 21 '80
   Dealing with adult illiteracy; study commissioned by the Ford Foundation. USA Today 108:8-9 D '79
   Is illiteracy necessary? J. C. Cairns. il Atlas 26:43 F '79
   Literate U.S; study by J. R. Bormuth. Sci Am 240:78 Mr '79

your library. Many libraries will not have all 160 magazines indexed in the *Readers' Guide.*

The *Guide* is easy to use and is as complete a locator of general information on a subject as you will find anywhere. It is an important first step in finding out about anything.

Readers' Guide also indexes titles of books that have been reviewed, but it is not as thorough a source in this area as *Book Review Digest* (New York: Wilson, 1905 to date). This monthly index summarizes reviews of books (nontechnical) that have appeared in 75 periodicals since 1905. The issues are bound into one annual volume to which a cumulative subject and title index is added. (There is a five-year-cumulative subject and title index as well.) Entries give the overall critical opinion of the book cited, then quote excerpts from the various reviews. A complete reference to the magazines in which it was reviewed is given, so you can locate the full reviews yourself. If you want to find out how a book fared, you'd consult the author/title index or find the date of publication from your library's card catalog, then go to that year's volume of *Book Review Digest.* Most libraries of over medium size subscribe to the index.

If you are digging for information in magazines appearing before 1900, the most widely used source which your library is likely to have is *Poole's Index to Periodical Literature, 1802-1907* (Boston: Houghton, Mifflin Company, 1891. Reprinted by Peter Smith, New York, 1938). The first magazine index to be published, *Poole's* indexes 470 American and British periodicals, by subject only. Book reviews are included. A microform reference to nineteenth century periodicals, *American Periodical Index 1728-1850,* edited by Nelson F. Adkins (New York: Readex, 1963) might be of use in scholarly searches. You are more likely to find this reference in a large public or university research library.

There are hundreds of other guides and indexes to periodicals which treat specific subjects or genres of work or regional materials. Some are *the* mainstays of reference work in a given field (*Index to Legal Periodicals; Art Index;* and *Business Periodicals Index,* for example); others are more general compilations but contain material not found in *Readers' Guide* or *Ulrich's.* See the Appendix for inclusion of these, by subject or area of interest.

NEWSPAPERS:
LISTS AND GUIDES

Consult your library's list of the newspapers it keeps on file (and the dates of issues) before using newspaper indexes or directories.

If you wish to know what newspapers are published in any city in the United States or if you want to find publication information (editors, price, address, circulation) about a specific newspaper, the source to go to is *Ayer Directory of Publications* (Philadelphia: N. W. Ayer & Son, Inc., 1880 to date). This annual directory contains information on 23,000 newspapers and magazines and the cities and towns in which they are published. Entries are arranged geographically. Your library will have a reference copy of *Ayers.* If the newspapers you want to locate were published before 1936, your best source would be *American Newspapers, 1821–1936; A Union List,* Winifred Gregory, ed. (New York: Wilson, 1937).

The major indexes to articles within newspapers are these: First, the *New York Times Index* (New York: New York Times, 1913 to date) should be one of your early steps in finding out about a subject. The *New York Times* comes as close as is possible to being *the* American newspaper, and your local library will have its *Index* and back issues, the latter on microfilm. It bears repeating that you can glean information from the *Index* alone, without ever having to go back to an original article. The entries are *that* complete.

The *Index* is issued semimonthly with an annual cumulation. Its volumes go back to 1851. Individuals and subjects are arranged alphabetically within, and under each subject heading events are ordered chronologically for that year. The entry events are ordered chronologically for that year. The entry then gives date, page, and column number of the original articles and a concise summary of each one. (The *Index* is a good way to simply find out the exact date on which an event took place.)

If it's business and finance articles you must search, a guide worth trying (if your library has it) is the *Wall Street Journal Index* (Princeton: Dow Jones Books, Inc., 1950 to date). The *New York Times* will have coverage of the major events in the world of business, but the *Wall Street Journal* provides the additional coverage of what it calls "Corporate News." Articles from 1950 on are indexed here, monthly, with an annual cumulation.

Eight major American newspapers are indexed in *Newspaper Index* (Wooster, Ohio: Bell & Howell, 1972 to date), going back to 1972. Each index is on one of the newspapers and contains a subject and personal-name list of the original article. The newspapers covered are: *The Washington Post; Los Angeles Times; Chicago Tribune; San Francisco Chronicle; Houston Post; The New Orleans Times Picayune; Detroit News;* and the *Milwaukee Journal.*

Recognizing a need to index local newspaper publications, many librarians have done this on their own. You should inquire as to whether your library has such a work. One recent guide to local newspaper indexes is *Newspaper Indexes: A Location and Subject Guide* (Metuchen, N.J.: Scarecrow Press, 1977), which arranges material by states.

Other major newspaper indexes you will find in many public and private libraries are: Times (London), *Index to the Times* (London: London Times, 1907 to date) a bimonthly guide to articles from 1906 to the present, by subject; the *Christian Science Monitor Index* (Wooster, Ohio: Bell & Howell, 1961 to date), ostensibly a religious paper, but well known for its national coverage and top-caliber editorial writing; and the *National Observer Index* (Princeton, N.J.: Dow Jones, 1969–

date), a guide to that weekly's articles arranged by subject and name headings. These will provide solid back-up to your use of the *New York Times Index*.

THE VERTICAL FILE

A vertical file means any material that can't stand up on shelves and is therefore stored vertically, usually in folders. The one in your library might hold anything that is not a book, magazine, newspaper or microform. There is no way of knowing without asking the librarian.

In general, however, the file will contain newspaper clippings, pamphlets, and booklets, which may have come from corporations, public or private associations, and/or government agencies. Any material your library thinks is not worth having bound will remain loose in these files, usually arranged alphabetically, by subject.

The *Vertical File Index* (New York: Wilson, 1935 to date) is a monthly general guide to the kinds of materials you might find in those drawers. Organized by subject, it gives brief descriptions of various kinds of materials one might expect to find; and many government and public affairs catalogues will refer you to publications kept in the vertical file. Still, there's no better way of finding out what's in there than asking a librarian or exploring the drawers on your own.

DISSERTATIONS AND REPORTS: USING ABSTRACTS AND INDEXES

Depending on the depth of your research and the narrowness of your subject, you may want to search such nonbound materials as dissertations and research reports. If your work is scientific or technical, you will certainly find these to be lucrative sources of information. Most of these materials are located through abstracting services.

An abstract service is like an index, except its material is often not organized by subject but rather by some other system (assigned numbers, type of publisher, or any kind of classification system). It is more valuable than an index, as it provides a summary (abstract) of the information contained in the original document. The *New York Times Index* is a quasi-abstract. Abstracts may be no more than a hundred words, but these give a succinct outline of the report, dissertation or study paper. Reading an abstract gives you a good indication of whether you want to take the time and money to obtain the entire information source.

Abstracts usually focus on a narrow subject area, which is why there are so many of them in the sciences. Many abstracting services are now parts of data base systems and, if available, this can prove an even quicker method of scanning information. Abstracts may include books and periodicals, but most of the material will be in "looser" form. Once you have consulted the abstracting service, using its index to find the subject heading that pertains to your topic, you go to the volume noted. By reading the abstract you can decide whether you want to obtain the entire article or paper. If you do, your first step is to check your library's card catalog and list of periodicals. It is always possible that the material will be there. More likely, though, you will have to order a photocopy or microform of the original document. The front of the abstracting service catalog will tell you how to go about it.

There are many abstracting services. The one that is perhaps of most interest to the nontechnical searcher is a monthly series, *Dissertation Abstracts International* (DAI) (Ann Arbor, Mich.: University Microfilms International, 1969 to date). DAI abstracts over 30,000 doctoral and masters' theses on many subjects, which have been accepted by American and Canadian universities (some European schools as well). The abstracts go back to 1938, prior to which date you must consult *Comprehensive Dissertation Index, 1861–1972* (Ann Arbor, Mich.: University Microfilms International, 1973), which lists over 400,000 dissertations.

The abstracts in DAI are arranged, first, by broad subject area. You'll see shelves of orange DAI catalogs marked "A," for instance; these contain abstracts in the humanities and social sciences. "B" catalogs cover the sciences; and "C," European abstracts. Then, within each of these broad areas, you'll find further subdivisions (for the social sciences, for example, there are Accounting, Biography, Sociology, and so on); and then still smaller categories within these (under Sociology are Criminology, Family, Labor Relations, etc.). These categories are listed in the table of contents, making the volumes easy to use. However, the primary tool of reference to DAI is the key-word title and author index found at the back of each volume, plus an author index included in each annual cumulation.

Figure 6–4 is an abstract taken from DAI. It was located by looking up the key-word "Credit" in the index. The index entry itself can give you an idea of what material will be found in the abstract. Then, once you've read the abstract, you'll be well versed in all aspects of the original dissertation. You'll certainly know whether you want to read it or not. At the end of the abstract is an order number, which you use to request a copy of the dissertation from University Microfilms, the publisher of DAI. Prices for photocopies vary, but you can expect to pay in the range of $20 to $25.

A dissertation can be an important resource in a search precisely because it deals with a narrowly defined subject. The first question to ask one's self in any information search is, "Has anyone done this identical search before?" If anyone has, you will save a lot of time and trouble by finding out who it was, then using their work as a reference and starting point for your own. An abstract can also be a quick method of filling in statistical or updated information when writing a speech, report, or article on a specific small topic.

Another important searching tool for information that is not bound is the Public Affairs Information Service's index, *Bulletin* (referred to as PAIS), (New York: Public Affairs Information Service, 1915 to date). PAIS is a subject index to

CREDIT RISK COMPENSATION: AN EMPIRICAL STUDY OF INVESTOR RETURN AND AGENCY RATINGS Order No. 8004145 BUSSA, ROBERT GENE, PH.D. *University of Illinois at Urbana-Champaign,* 1979. 146pp.

In recent years, the use of bond ratings as indicators of credit risk has come under strong criticism for a variety of reasons. The first major criticism rests on the contention that the bond market is a more efficient rater of bonds than rating agencies, i.e., the market better anticipates fundamental changes in financial positions of firms. The second criticism is that of rating agency's lack of statistical rigor in the determination of risk and the possible bias inherent in subjective methods of evaluation. This study investigates whether credit risk as estimated by rating agencies represents credit risk as perceived by investors in the bond market.

A model developed by Bryan and Carlton is used to directly estimate certainty coefficients for bonds rated Aaa to Baa (by Moody's) for various seven-year periods. These certainty coefficients are then used to examine the risks associated with bonds in the various rating categories.

The results of this analysis are similar to those obtained by Silvers. However, there are two interesting departures which deserve special attention. First, the differences in the certainty coefficients of A and Baa rated bonds are not significantly different for nine of the 14 coefficients generated. Also, the difference between the average risk premium of A and Baa bonds is extremely small, if not zero. This lack of difference may be attributed to the time periods studied and the relatively short maturities. However, the lack of difference may be due to a similarity in perceived risk. If so, the similarity in perceived risk suggests that investors independently evaluate the creditworthiness of each bond as opposed to totally accepting the judgments of rating services. In contrast to the findings of Katz, the bond market may indeed be efficient with respect to bonds rated as lower quality. Aaa and Aa rated securities generally have distinct levels of perceived risk.

The second departure is present in the certainty coefficients themselves. While Silvers' estimation technique presents a smoothly declining set of certainty coefficients, this study generated fluctuating certainty coefficients. These results might be a function of the data used or the use of the term structure of interest as opposed to yields to maturity.

periodicals, pamphlets, government documents and varying other loose forms of material in the fields of economics, political science, government and international affairs. It also indexes legislation as it is published. Like the *Readers' Guide,* PAIS is published weekly, then cumulated four times throughout the year until an annual volume is issued. Many libraries will just have the annual volumes. You can approach PAIS directly by looking under its broad subject areas, which are arranged alphabetically, in each annual or more recent issue, or you may refer to it through a printed work, *The Cumulative Subject Index to the PAIS Annual Bulletin 1915-1974* (Arlington, Va.: Carrollton Press, Inc., 1975), but then you will still have to go to the regular annual index for the appropriate citation; or if you have access, you may search PAIS through on its own data base. If your subject in any way involves government or political affairs, you should check PAIS at some stage of your research.

There are abstracting and indexing services for all fields. Some may be searched on data bases as well as through published catalogs; others are indexed only in print. A few of the key printed abstract or indexing services are: *Psychological Abstracts* (Washington, D.C.: American Psychological Association, 1927–date); *Applied Science and Technology Index* (New York: H. W. Wilson Company, 1958 to date); *America: History and Life; Part A., Article Abstracts and Citations* (Santa Barbara, Cal.: American Bibliographical Center–Clio Press, 1974); and *Resources in Education* (Washington, D.C.: Government Printing Office, 1966 to date). This last is the giant in the education field and part of an enormous specialized information system called ERIC which can search almost everything written in the field, through its own data base. ERIC can search related abstracts, such as *Psychological Abstracts* as well. It is a "must" information resource for anyone in education.

To find out if there's an abstract or index in your field, you can consult either a general reference book guide, such as Bohdan Wynar's *American Reference Books Annual* (Littleton, Col.: Libraries Unlimited, Inc., 1970 to date) or

An interview with Zbigniew Brze-
zinski [on the Iranian and
Afghanistan crises]. il *Wall St J*
195:20 Ja 15 '80

BUDGET, BUSINESS

Houck, Lewis Daniel, jr. A practical
guide to budgetary and management control systems: a functional
and performance evaluation approach. '79 xix + 234p tables
charts index (LC 78-14716) (ISBN
0-669-02705-7) $21.95 *—Lexing-*
ton bks.;—Heath Can

BUDGET, GOVERNMENT

Year of the farmer? [comments on
and summary of the Thailand
draft budget for 1980]. il tables
charts *Bangkok Bank Mo R*
20:401-16 O/N '79

BUILDING

Regulation
Bibliography

McGowan, Anne. Government regulations and the cost of housing:
a partially annotated bibliography.
N '79 11p bibl (CPL bibl no.
18) $3.50 *— Council planning*
librarians

BUSINESS INFORMATION

Brudney, Victor. Insiders, outsiders,
and informational advantages under the federal securities laws
[extent to which securities laws,
which restrain corporate insiders from trading on the basis
of inside information, can be
applied to outsiders who may
possess informational advantages].
Harvard Law R 93:322-76 D '79

BUSINESS MEN

Howell, James M. Shifting patterns
in southern business leadership
[based on information about
business leaders listed in the 1951
and 1977 editions of Who's who].
tables *R Regional Econ and Bus*
4:3-9 O '79

**BUSINESS ORGANIZATION AND
ADMINISTRATION**

†Scott, William G. and David K. Hart.
Organizational America. '79 xv + 272p
table charts index (LC 79-13815)
(ISBN 0-395-27599-7) $11.95 *—*
Houghton
Jacket subtitle: Can individual
freedom survive within the security it
promises.

Figure 6-5. From Public Affairs Information Service, *Bulletin,* January 1,
1980. Vol. 66, No. 7. Reprinted with permission of Public Affairs Information
Service. Copyright © 1980 Public Affairs Information Service.

Eugene P. Sheehy's *Guide to Reference Books,* 9th ed.
(Chicago: American Library Association, 1976), one of which
most libraries will have; or simply ask your librarian, who receives notice of new abstracting and indexing services on an
ongoing basis. (See the list by subject of reference materials in
the Appendix of this book, which includes abstracting and
indexing sources.) In addition, a good general guide to bibli-

ographies of dissertations and the like is Michael M. Reynolds, ed., *Guide to Theses and Dissertations* (Detroit: Gale, 1975). Keep in mind, though, that there are new services being born almost daily, making printed guides soon obsolete.

Abstracting and indexing services include much of the published work of research centers. But still some research and development work is constantly "in progress" or otherwise unpublished. For this reason you need a backup source to the indexing services; the best one is the *Research Centers Directory,* referred to many times in this book. Once you have identified an organization or institution doing research on the topic you're interested in, you should query them directly about their printed reports or working papers.

MICROFORMS

Most reference material is in printed forms. But as libraries fight the battle against shrinking shelf space and more published information, the use of other forms to store material becomes widespread.

Microforms means books (or other print forms) that have been "shrunk" into a yet smaller form, which can then be read only through a machine that enlarges (called a "reader"). The most commonly used microform is microfilm, and almost all libraries — no matter how small — have some information stored in this form. A microfilm reader is easy to use: You operate it by hand, turning levers to move the reel of film from one spool to another. As the film passes under a lens (through which light streams), an enlarged image of the "page" appears on the screen. You focus by hand to your own vision. Many microfilm readers now include a copier-printing function so that you can focus on the page you need, insert money, and have your own copy to keep. The information you are apt to find on microfilm is: back issues of newspapers, particularly the *New York Times;* small, specialized journals and periodicals; and, depending on the size of your library, doctoral dissertations and published reports.

Microfiche is another microform whose use is growing, even in smaller collections. Transparent sheets of film, actually four-by-six inch cards, are run through a reader much like the one used for microfilm. Each card holds approximately 70 pages (which have been reduced, of course) of printed information. Again, you adjust focus and finder by hand. Many microfiche readers also have copying-printing functions. Material you might find on fiche in your library are: back issues of newspapers, journals, any out-of-print books that are part of your library's special collection, and, increasingly, government reports and documents.

Similar data is also stored on microcards, although these are not yet common in local libraries. The cards are like microfiche — they store about the same amount of pages on each card — but are not transparent and thus require yet another type of machine reader.

The best way to find out what a particular library stores on microform is to ask. The best way to find out what is out there and available, although not in your library, is to consult *Guide to Microforms in Print* (Weston, Conn.: Microform Review, 1961 to date). The guide is issued annually and lists over 60,000 titles, although it does not include theses or dissertations. There is a companion *Subject Guide to Microforms in Print,* which may prove of even greater use. Call libraries in your community until you find one that has those volumes. A public library, if small, may not have them, while a smaller but more specialized collection that relies on micro storage undoubtedly will.

PICTURES

If you've ever had to plan a book, report, or printed promotional piece you know that pictures can indeed be worth a thousand words of information; in some cases they are important assets to presenting other kinds of information.

One way to obtain pictures is to hire a picture researcher (see Chapter Eight on Professional Researchers), and if your project is a large one, you may want to choose that route. But even if you never have to do your own picture research, you should be aware of what is out there and available in the form of pictures, photographs, and illustrations.

Pictures may come from books or periodicals or they may have been drawn, painted, or photographed directly, then reproduced in a form that can be used (by you) for print materials. In either case, having the picture in the original book won't do you much good; you'll have to obtain the reproduction yourself in order to reprint it in your form.

Reproductions lie chiefly in general libraries, picture libraries (which may be owned by private businesses, associations, or public institutions), and photograph stock houses.

Assuming you have a general idea of the subject you wish to illustrate, try to narrow down in your mind what a "perfect" single illustration of that subject might be, if it existed. You will no doubt have to make do with a less-than-perfect alternative, but if you can begin with as specific a requirement as possible, your search will be easier.

If you know of a picture collection that relates specifically to your subject, then you're home free; but if there isn't one, your first stop should be at whatever public picture collections there are in your town. Look through the *American Library Directory* and note the picture collection capabilities of libraries in your area. A large public library will probably have its own picture collection, arranged by subject, in a separate room or branch. The *Directory* will tell you which library does and where it is located. Specialized libraries may have separate catalogs and indexes to their picture collections or they may simply store them by some assigned subject arrangement in file drawers. Call librarians and ask for particulars about their collections. When looking through the *Directory* pay special attention to museum libraries, as they often have extensive picture and slide files as well as facilities for reproducing them. And don't overlook the Library of Congress (see p. 88) as one excellent source of pictures, no matter how far you are from Washington, D.C.

The classified or yellow pages of your city's telephone directory is another starting point for finding picture libraries. Because the line between a photographic stock house and a picture library is a thin, often vague one, you should check both subject headings, "Photographs–Stock" and "Picture Libraries." Needless to say, the major ones are in Manhattan. They serve customers throughout the country, however, and are set up to process queries quickly and efficiently. Many have charge accounts, overnight delivery, and other aids to the distant picture searcher. The very well-known ones, used by professional and nonprofessional researchers, are: Bettmann Archive, Inc., 136 East 57th Street, New York, N.Y. 10022; Culver Pictures Inc., 660 First Avenue, New York, N.Y. 10016; Glove Photos Inc, 404 Park Avenue South, New York, N.Y. 10016; and the Granger Collection, 1841 Broadway, New York, N.Y. 10023 (whose catalog *Some Pictures from the Past: A Guide to the Granger Collection* you should request). These houses have millions (millions, literally; Culver alone has approximately nine million separate items) of photographs, prints, drawings, on every subject available for reproduction. (Other picture collections are included in the Appendix list of reference materials, by subject area.)

Photograph houses and libraries also have themselves listed in special directories that serve particular industries. *Literary Market Place* (New York: Bowker, 1978), the publishing industry's annual directory of services and providers, is available at most libraries. The book has a section "Photo and Picture Sources," which details all kinds of picture services, including the names and specialties of photographers who will take pictures for you.

Unfortunately, there is no good single guide to what is out there in illustrations and pictures. Real searching by you or someone else in your employ is required.

OTHER NONPRINT MATERIALS

If you were to visit a typical public high school in America, you'd see the entire gamut of nonprint informational material, from microform reader to computer terminal. Some of the forms within this range have been traditionally used in schools and only recently have moved into libraries and businesses. There are published guides to these materials, but most are either designed for school use or cover only one form — films, for instance. A work you might want to look at is *Museum Media* (Detroit: Gale, 1973–date), a directory of print and audiovisual materials published by museums, art galleries and historical societies and collections. All American and Canadian institutions are arranged alphabetically with a list of their publications and prices. An index to the titles and key-words of all publications and to subject and place of all institutions is included.

Another — probably the best — route to audio-visual material is, again, through the *American Library Directory,* looking up the libraries in your community. In some cases, entries will describe such material in great detail ("special patents collection available on microfiche"). Where you are not certain, call up the library. The forms you will encounter, in addition to microforms, are these: cassettes, filmstrips, charts, records, tapes, maps and relief models, slides and transparencies, motion pictures, photographs, and a myriad of video forms (tapes and cassettes but with sound as well as picture), called "audio visual" or "A/V equipment" by libraries.

DATA BASES

The computer has opened up information gathering possibilities that were unheard of twenty years ago. The past few years have seen computer information retrieval move away from the exclusive province of big business and into the offices of libraries, small enterprises, government agencies, and even the homes of private individuals. It is thus not inconceivable that within a few years, Americans will use computer terminals to get information in much the same way that they now use corner pay telephone booths to reach people: Drop in a dollar and search a data base.

In the meantime, one has to come to terms with the state of the art of data bases if they are to be included in one's research battery and that means, first, understanding the language with which "information retrieval" surrounds and often mythologizes itself. It is not a difficult science to apply, and one need not understand the science to use its product.

A data base is a collection of information, or data, that usually deals with a specific subject. The information has been organized so that you can search it directly yourself via a computer-linked keyboard, or you can have it searched for you through a telephone hook-up. The latter approach is called being "on-line." Many of the largest and most useful data bases are now available on an on-line basis. This kind of information retrieval is fast: In a standard search of bibliographic indexes, for example, the computer can search as many as one million references in one minute.

Data bases are prepared by both public and private organizations. Some are only for in-house use, that is, for the staff of a company or association. However, most are for rent or have made some arrangement for public use.

The actual information in the data base is not new, much of it a mere duplication of what is already written somewhere — in journals, indexes, abstracting services, bibliographies, or other standard reference sources. The *New York Times,* for instance, prepares and markets a data base that is primarily the information you find in the large red volumes of the *New York Times Index* in your library. *Dissertations Abstracts International* is part of a data base called Comprehensive Dissertation Index, and PAIS and *America: History and Life* are two other abstracts cited earlier that are available on-line as well as in print. Occasionally, data bases are entirely statistical: A firm may have prepared its own data base of production figures, inventory costs or other numerical information that it needs to get at quickly and often. The U.S. Census Bureau stores much of its material on a data base. Still other data bases serve as dictionaries for specific professions or fields: The CHEMLINE base, which stores generic and common names and the molecular formulas for chemical substances, is one example.

Data base systems, also called data banks, are merely groupings of two or more data bases together. Companies rent you access, through on-line hookups, to systems that may contain as many as 50 individual data bases. Since the same data base may be on more than one system, an on-line user would want to hook up with the system that offered the greatest number and best mix of bases for his or her field. For example, the data base Comprehensive Dissertation Index is offered by three systems, but only one of the three also offers the National Library of Medicine's data base, MEDLARS. The other two systems do not.

Several data bases are not a part of any system. NEW YORK TIMES INFORMATION BANK (a data base of information from the *New York Times* and 70 other newspapers and periodicals) and POPINFORM (articles, reports, proceedings, unpublished papers and theses on the subject of fertility control) are two examples.

The three major data base systems are:

Bibliographic Retrieval Services, Inc. (BRS)
Corporation Park, Building 702
Goshen, New York 12302 (518)374–5011

Lockheed Information System (Dialog)
3251 Hanover Street
Palo Alto, California 94304 and
200 Park Avenue, Suite 303 East
New York, New York 10017 (212)682–4630

System Development Corporation
2500 Colorado Avenue
Santa Monica, California 90406 and
SDC Search Service
401 Hackensack Avenue
Hackensack, New Jersey 07601 (201)487-0571

Individual data bases are also included in the Appendix list of reference materials by subject area.

When you use a data base *directly* (which you will not be doing in all likelihood), you "ask" it for information by phrasing your question in terms that correspond to the base's headings (or "descriptors"), under which information has been arranged. If you were to ask, "What's been written in the past ten years on the subject of government regulation of municipal bond offerings?" you would have to use the descriptors employed by the particular data base. "Municipal bonds" would no doubt be one; "federal government" another; and there would be a separate descriptor for your time requirement (ten years). Key-wording a computerized information retrieval system is not unlike the key-wording done by a researcher when he or she begins a project. If you can't break down your queries into descriptors at the start, you'll have difficulty describing what you're searching for to any information system, be it computer, librarian, or printed index.

In response to your query, the computer returns to you citations, references to specific articles (or whatever kind of source is stored in the data base), with dates, volume and page numbers, and perhaps a one-line headline or summarizing sentence as well. The computer will also tell you the exact descriptors under which the information was located. Some of these you may not have thought of and they may provide you with additional clues to a future related search. You perhaps recognize already that the material received from the computer is not unlike the material you'd find in a printed abstract or bibliography. This method is faster.

How do you gain access to a data base? First of all,

your own company may have access. Ask the librarian or supervisor of whatever research function is performed within your firm. Another way is to go on-line yourself: Rent a terminal that is hooked up to whichever data base(s) you need. If you require several of the major systems, you will need more than one terminal. An average terminal will cost several hundred dollars a month, and you will also be billed by the systems company for search time, usually on a monthly basis. Search time costs between 75¢ and $3.00 per minute. Only a professional researcher or someone paid to work full-time on a lengthy research project will find this route expeditious.

A third way is to go through a retailer, a firm that does research for a fee and is on-line to the systems you wish to use. (See Chapter Eight for descriptions of such firms and the kinds of services they provide.) You can expect to pay about $40 per hour (depending on the difficulty and extent of search), plus the actual search time charged by the data base system.

A few private or public offices with on-line access will let certain individuals use their services. Occasionally, large law firms will let outsiders search their services for a fee. It helps pay their cost overhead on the terminal. Such firms are likely to have the NEW YORK TIMES INFORMATION BANK and LEXIS, which stores all state and federal statutory law in the United States. For your future reference, call the largest firm in your town and ask if they have on-line access to any data bases and whether anyone may use their service for a fee. Colleges and universities in your area may also have such services, helping to pay for their cost overhead. Graduate schools in the sciences are a particularly good bet for being on-line to the many scientific and technical data bases.

More and more public libraries are investing in access to information retrieval systems, too; but they must usually band together to afford it. In the New York metropolitan area a group of public, college, and private business libraries have joined through METRO (the New York Metropolitan Reference and Research Library Agency) to provide access to the major data base systems. But it doesn't mean that you, the individual user, therefore have direct access. You would still go through a reference librarian with your query; and only if the information were unobtainable by standard research routes or of the kind that would be more efficiently obtained by computer, would the METRO librarian be asked to conduct the search for you. Still, it is worth knowing if your local library system has any provision whatsoever for such access and what the procedures are for using it.

Then there are a number of government or quasi-public agencies and organizations that will allow certain persons to search their systems. The Department of Defense will let contractors and other potential suppliers search its data base; the New York State Office of Drug Abuse Services will allow individuals working in that field to use its SDC and DIALOG systems; The Foundation Center (888 Seventh Avenue, New York, N.Y. 10019), which has SDC and DIALOG as well as the NEW YORK TIMES INFORMATION BANK, also has its own base that stores descriptions of more than 2,500 foundations and the grants they make each year. You may not search the Center's bases directly, but you may buy selected printouts of the information retrieved from the base.

Several agencies within the federal government will have on-line access not available to the general public but perhaps still available to you, the researcher. If you've taken the hints in Chapter Three as to finding experts within such agencies, you may find yourself in a position to make use of the expert's research resources. The data base system is one of these resources.

And, finally, there is the ever valuable Library of Congress. Its computer capabilities are useful to you if you're looking for bibliographic material. While official library policy is that a search will be made only through written application to the General Reading Room Division, the fact is that terminals are located in the building (where you can actually get your hands on them yourself, if you are willing to spend time figuring out how to use them) and searches are often conducted in response to telephone queries. In addition to its Bibliographic Information File data base and its catalog of books, the Library also has on data base the National Referral Center's Master List (see p. 45) of scientific experts willing to answer queries.

There is no one complete guide to data bases or data base systems. Developments in the information processing field proceed so rapidly that as soon as information is published it is superseded by newer information. One general guide to the subject, which many libraries will have, is the *Encyclopedia of Information Systems and Services,* Anthony T. Kruzas, ed., 2nd International edition (Ann Arbor, Mich.: Anthony T. Kruzas Associates, 1974). The book lists the publishers and organizations that specialize in quick-access services and identifies various data bases and abstracting-indexing services by subject. Again, note, that it will be outdated to some degree.

If you think you may have need to investigate specific data bases that relate to your work, a better idea is to obtain a "miscellaneous publication" of METRO, the New York Metropolitan Reference and Research Library Agency (33 West 42nd Street, New York, N.Y. 10036). An eighty-page pamphlet, *Directory of Libraries Providing Computer-Based Information Services in the New York Metropolitan Area; A Selected List, 1978,* is more universally applicable than its title indicates. Apart from its New York listing, the guide describes in detail the contents of the major individual data bases in all fields, tells which are a part of which systems, and where in the New York area on-line access may be had. The *Directory* costs $10.00 and may be ordered from METRO. Another approach to this information would be to write the major data base system providers themselves.

The value to you of using a data base depends on the kind of information you seek and the amount of time it would otherwise take you to find it. Data bases are not the perfect answer to the researcher's needs. For one thing, their expense at this stage makes them infeasible as an everyday resource; for another, they are basically duplicates of information already organized and printed by human beings, which means the quality of their information is no better or worse than the person or persons who prepared the index, abstract, bibliography, or other data source. In many bases, the computer does not give you the original information but merely a reference or citation to that information source. If it's an abstract, you still have to locate the original article and purchase it in a printed form. The computer can only lead you to it more quickly. It is precisely the time factor that makes computerized searching either worthwhile or a mere extravagance. You are not necessarily the best determinant of whether you need computer searching. If you're considering using this kind of reference material, be sure to explore the field thoroughly first. Talk to the people who use information retrieval systems — librarians and professional researchers — and know what they can and cannot do.

7

government information

The United States Government Printing Office (GPO) publishes approximately 20,000 documents each year. Individual federal agencies, commissions, Congressional committees, and quasi-public commissions and study groups print thousands more; and then there are the state, county, and local governments as well. You will never need most of these publications, but you should know that government — particularly the federal government — is a prime information source on any subject. If you know what kinds of information are available, you'll be able to tap this resource quickly, efficiently, and creatively.

It helps to know jargon and policies straightaway. Government publishing often means lengthy titles (of people, institutions, and publications) and a plethora of abbreviations. GPO (the Government Printing Office), GAO (the Government Accounting Office) and SuDoc Number (the classification number of every government publication, which is assigned by the Superintendent of Documents in the GPO) are the key ones to remember. For most publications the Superintendent of Documents is the "author" and the GPO the publisher. Each publication has an ordering number as well as a SuDoc number, and your dealings with the GPO will be far simpler if you can provide both numbers, as well as titles, in your correspondence. Where at all possible, try to avoid ordering through the GPO in Washington.

If you wish to understand the field at large before approaching individual indexes and lists of government publications, there are books worth studying. Joe Morehead's *Introduction to United States Public Documents* (Littleton, Col.: Libraries Unlimited, 1975) is a textbook that details and explores the functions of the major agencies and their publications; it provides a lot of information on the government-as-publisher as well. Laurence F. Schmeckebier and Roy B. Eastin's *Government Publications and Their Use*, 2nd rev. ed. (Washington, D.C.: The Brookings Institution, 1969) is an older but still relevant overview of how to obtain and use government sources of information. One directory of particular relevance to business and economic researchers is *Washington Information Workbook*, 1979 ed. (Washington, D.C.: Washington Researchers, 1979). This 300-page handbook gives names, telephone numbers and descriptions of valuable — many are little-known — information sources within the federal government. The volume is not inexpensive ($35 for the 1979 edition) so you may want to check a public business library or a corporation library before ordering a copy.

Of course, you don't really have to have any of these books. The essential government publication that will help you understand what's available is the current edition of the *United States Government Manual* (mentioned early in this book). That volume will give an overview of government functions, and easily make you aware of which agencies are responsible for which subjects. You can buy the *Manual* for $6.50 at any U.S. Government Bookstore (look up "U.S. Government" in your telephone book to find out if your city has one) or order it through the GPO itself.

The other staples of federal publications, available at local government bookstores are these: *The Budget of the U.S. Government* (for the current fiscal year), $4.00;

Appendix to the Budget of the U.S. Government, $13.00; the most current annual edition of the *Official Congressional Directory,* paperback, $6.50 (see p. 139 for details); and the *Statistical Abstract of the United States,* paperback, $8.50 (see p. 138 for details). One additional basic volume of note is *The Public Papers of the Presidents,* an annual compilation of presidential speeches, news conferences, and other material released by the White House during the year. The above come under the heading of basic reference works, and would be most useful only to someone whose work focused on government as a subject (though the *Directory* and *Statistical Abstract* can be valuable sources to nongovernment researchers).

But suppose you are beginning to gather information for a project for which you have no previous expertise, and you don't know yet which part of the government, if any, can be of help. While still in the primary stage of your research, you would do well to check the *Monthly Catalog of United States Government Publications* (Washington, D.C.: Government Printing Office, 1895 to date), which you'll find at any major public or school library. The *Catalog* lists almost all documents made public by the Government in the twentieth century. An annual index (there is a six-month cumulative index as well) is easy to use; you approach it by either author, title, or subject. The subject headings are like the ones you'd find in your library's card catalog — they make sense. The index refers you by entry number to a page, on which the publications are listed with their documents classification numbers. Note the SuDoc number at once, as you will need it to order the publication either from the GPO in Washington or from your local Government Bookstore.

There is also now available a privately published index to the *Catalog,* which saves your having to check each annual volume's index: *Cumulative Subject Index to the Monthly Catalog of U.S. Government Publications, 1900-1971* compiled by William Buchanan and Edna A. Kanely (Washington, D.C.: Carrollton Press, 1973-1975) indexes publications by subject for those years, with annual supplements for the years

Figure 7-1. From the *Monthly Catalog of United States
Government Publications,* May 1978, Number 10002.
Reprinted with permission of Superintendent of Docu-
ments, U.S. Government Printing Office.

after 1971. Or, you can try one of the more popularly written
guides to the *Monthly Catalog,* such as the *Monthly Catalog of
United States Government Publications: An Introduction to Its
Use,* by John Gordon Burke and Carol Dugan Wilson (Hamden,
Conn.: Linnet Books, 1973).

If your library is one of the officially designated
U.S. Government documents depositories, it may have many
of the original publications listed in the *Catalog.* That, too,
would save you the time of ordering through Washington; so
ask the librarian. The materials might be in the vertical file or
shelved in a more organized fashion in sections of their own.

Selected U.S. Government Publications

The *Monthly Catalog* may have everything, but do
you need to know everything that is out there? There are times
when a selective list arranged for easy access is more helpful.

The Public Affairs Information Service's (PAIS) *Bulletin* (see p. 113) will often be a more useful instrument for locating government material than the *Monthly Catalog*. The *Index to U.S. Government Periodicals* (Chicago: Infordata International, 1974 to date) falls into the same category. It is a smaller — but sufficient for most purposes — guide to what exists in the federal-publication field, covering 150 periodicals issued by the various agencies. Entries are indexed by subject and author in this quarterly publication, with an annual cumulation. You'll find the *Index* in large libraries, government reference libraries or libraries affiliated with schools of law or public administration.

The GPO also issues a guide to its most popular and most frequently ordered publications. Even a small library is likely to have *Selected U.S. Government Publications* (Washington, D.C., Government Printing Office, 1928 to date), which comes out monthly (except for twice a year when combined issues appear) and describes, by general subject heading, those publications expected to have greatest popular appeal. Taxes, social security, and infant care are among the all-time best-sellers, but the lists include many that are more specialized. You may want to subscribe to the list yourself so as to keep abreast of what is available in the government's information warehouse.

A new addition to the government's battery of information for the lay person is *The Consumer Information Catalog*, which originates in the Consumer Information Center, General Services Administration, in Pueblo, Colorado 81009. The Pueblo center has been set up for consumer publications exclusively and provides another way of avoiding the Washington logjam of GPO orders. The *Catalog* is published quarterly, containing about 15 pages of booklet descriptions, by such subject arrangement as Employment and Education; Health; and Housing. Many of the booklets are free; the remainder usually cost under $1.

Another site of federally generated information outside the GPO ordering axis is the Government Accounting Office (GAO). That office is empowered to issue reports on an enormous range of government activities — financial, accounting, audits and reviews, studies and investigations. You may obtain most of these reports for $1. A *Monthly List of GAO Reports* can be had free by writing to the GAO, 441 G Street, N.W., Washington, D.C. 20548.

The National Technical Information Service (NTIS) is a central clearinghouse for scientific and technical information, particularly government-funded research and development reports, analyses and studies. NTIS has a standing publication list of almost one million titles. If you think there could be a report for a topic you're researching — and there probably will be one — there are several ways to approach NTIS.

First, you may consult its own biweekly abstract service, *Government Reports Announcements* (Springfield, Va.: National Technical Information Service, 1946 to date), copies of which will be in all federal depository libraries. Look under the broad subject category you're researching. There are about 25 subject categories, all scientific. If you prefer, you may look in the service's annual index, *Government Reports Index,* by subject or author. When you've located a report that interests you, read the abstract to find out if you'll want to obtain the full report. You can then purchase the original, either in paper or microfiche, from the agency's Information and Sales Center, 425 Thirteenth Street, N.W., Washington, D.C.

A second possible approach to NTIS material is via its computer search services. NTIS can custom-search the major data base systems for abstracts in all areas of the sciences, going back to 1964. For approximately $125, the search service will provide you with a bibliography of up to one hundred abstracts in your subject area.

That's the expensive route. A cheaper method is to find out if your subject falls within the over one thousand searches that NTIS has already published. Someone else may have performed your search already. NTIS-published searches include such topics as sea power plants, ocean waste disposal, tumor viruses, and human aggression (237 abstracts in this search). Contact NTIS Search Department by mail or telephone [(202)558-4642] and ask to be sent *PR-186 Published Search*

Catalog. All reports abstracted in such published searches may be purchased from the NTIS Sales Center, for approximately $30 each. For further details on NTIS' information services write or call: NTIS, U.S. Department of Commerce, 5285 Port Royal Road, Springfield, Virginia 22161.

The Securities and Exchange Commission is an information publisher, and will make available copies of the annual, quarterly, and special reports that U.S. companies must file with its office; the Federal Trade Commission publishes analyses of specific industries and companies; the Bureau of the Census does periodic surveys and reports on a wide range of subjects including business, housing, health, and education. And there are many more direct information sources within the various agencies and commissions. (See the Appendix, by subject, for more.) Where possible, try to order directly through the originating agency. You'll get what you want faster and perhaps cheaper.

Other direct information routes lie within the executive branch. The *United States Government Manual* will be a good indicator of whom to approach for what kinds of published information. In the manual, at the end of each agency's chapter, you'll find "Sources for Information." Several list pamphlets by name; others provide the name of a person to call for the specific names and titles of publications.

There are privately published guides to agency publications too. John Andriot's *Guide to U.S. Government Publications* (McLean, Va.: Documents Index, 1976–1978) is an annual service, which your library may receive. It gives a detailed list with descriptions of which publications are issued by some two thousand agencies. W. Philip Leidy's *A Popular Guide to Government Publications*, 4th ed. (New York: Columbia University Press, 1978) uses broad subject headings to describe popular-interest publications issued between 1967 and 1975. Ellen Jackson's *Subject Guide to Major United States Government Publications* (Chicago: American Library Assn., 1968) is another useful source. Other, more specialized guides are included in the Appendix lists.

Many of the agencies mentioned — Census Bureau, Commerce Department, Securities and Exchange Commission — generate statistics on selected subjects on a regular basis. However, for an overview of statistical data available from the government, there are several fundamental works to consult.

The Bureau of the Census's *Statistical Abstract of the United States* (Washington, D.C.: Government Printing Office, 1879 to date) is an annual summary of data on American economic, political, and social life. The book is a handy ready-reference work to own; and it gives complete citations for each table or chart used so that you can refer to the appropriate agency for the original, or more specific, data. The *Abstract* is available at every library, but you may buy it yourself in paperback for $8.50 at a Government Bookstore (or order through the GPO).

The Census Bureau is, naturally, a major provider of statistics. In addition to the *Abstract*, its most useful publications are: *County and City Data Book* (1952 to date), which provides categories of census information for all counties and cities with a population of over 25,000; the *Congressional District Data Book* (1961 to date), exceptionally useful in political campaigns, this volume shows population and housing data and votes cast by congressional district; and *Historical Statistics of the United States, Colonial Times to 1970*, a two-volume cumulation of the same kind of data that appears in the *Statistical Abstract* but here goes back, year by year, to the nation's beginning. A Government Bookstore will have all of these, or you can order through the GPO in Washington.

The *American Statistics Index* (Washington, D.C.: Congressional Information Service, 1973 to date) indexes and describes all statistical publications of federal agencies. The guide is an annual publication, but updates itself in monthly supplements. There are two volumes: the first is an "Index" (by subject, name, and category), which refers you to the second, an "Abstract", which describes the various publications and gives complete price and SuDoc number information. If you're looking for statistical data on a specific subject, the most current volume of the *American Statistics Index* is a good place to start. If your own library does not subscribe, call government offices and graduate school libraries until you find one that does. A helpful librarian can check the references for you over the telephone and give you the name of specific publications and originating agencies. Microfiche copies of original documents are also available from the *Index's* own service.

Congressional Publications

There are publications issued by Congress, and then there are publications about Congress. In the latter category the primary reference work is the official *Congressional Directory,* cited earlier in this book. You may purchase it through any Government Bookstore or directly through the Government Printing Office. In a paper edition, it costs $6.50. Even a small local library will have a copy, usually at the reference desk, as it is a work used frequently to answer queries. The *Directory* is published each year — editions date back to 1809 — and includes biographical sketches of all members of Congress (House and Senate) plus federal judges. Separate sections include maps of congressional districts, personnel lists of government agencies at certain levels, and accredited members of the Washington Press Corps.

The *Directory* does not give information on Congress's staff; for that information you might want to consult the *Congressional Staff Directory* (Alexandria,Va.: The Congressional Staff Directory, 1959 to date), which also comes out annually. This volume gives biographical information on the staff members of members of Congress, committees, and subcommittees, with addresses, assignments, and other particulars. It is not an essential addition to your reference shelf, as most libraries will have a copy and you can always call up a congressperson's office and ask for the name of the aide assigned to your topic of interest.

The *Biographical Directory of the American Congress, 1774-1971* (Washington, D.C.: Government Printing Office, 1971) provides short pieces on all Senators and Congresspersons who have served in the past, plus descriptions of cabinet members from George Washington's government up through Richard Nixon's. And one other very good, popularly written guide to members is the *Almanac of American Politics* (see p. 31), an updated version of which is published for each new Congress. The *Almanac* gives biographical information, facts about each state and Congressional district, votes by each member on selected key issues, ratings for each member by public-interest and other special-interest groups, and very savvy political analyses of the members' chances for reelection or higher political office. The *Almanac* is available in paper at many bookstores.

The official journal of Congress is the *Congressional Record* (Washington, D.C.: Government Printing Office, 1873 to date) which covers its proceedings on a daily basis. Speeches, actions taken on bills, remarks — the *Record* is a grabbag of names, laws, and jokes, a perpetuator of the myths and folklore of Congress. Entertaining, yes, but how useful will it be for you? It does not usually include the actual texts of bills and resolutions. And members are allowed to amend their speeches and remarks, so that there is some question as to how "authentic" the final result may be. The *Record's* index is printed every other week, with an annual cumulation as well. You may want to look through a sample of the *Record,* if only to know what it is; but there are better sources of information on the proceedings of Congress.

The quickest way to find out if there is pending legislation on a subject of interest to you is to call LEGIS, the Office of Legislative Information, (202)225-8646. (This office was formerly called the House Bill Status office.) Through its own data base, LEGIS can tell you which bills deal with your topic and then track their progress through Congress. If one of your bills is in committee — most are — you can contact a staff member of that committee for further information you might want — a copy of the bill, chances of its passage, or anything else you want to know.

Congressional Quarterly Weekly Report (Washington, D.C.: Congressional Quarterly, Inc., 1945 to date) is a useful print source, both in its weekly and almanac forms. The *Congressional Quarterly* is really a news service that summarizes the past week's events in Congress and other branches of the federal government. Each issue shows the status and progress of major legislation, charts committee and floor activity, and details the votes recorded. One week's issue will refer you to information in another issue, with adequate citations. Then, there is a separate index prepared quarterly, plus an annual cumulation, *Congressional Quarterly Almanac,* which provides a legislative roundup for the year. There are other private services similar to *Congressional Quarterly* but this is the one that libraries of even medium size will have. *Congressional Quarterly* material is also indexed in PAIS's *Bulletin* by subject category.

Congress, too, is a publisher of bills, hearings, and reports. Because the *Congressional Record* only covers that information in fragmentary fashion, an additional reference work is required. The Congressional Information Service's *Index to Publications of the United States Congress* (called CIS/Index) (Washington, D.C.: Congressional Information Service, 1970 to date) is a monthly service that meets the need. It is best approached through its annual editions. Most of the material published by Congress is indexed here by subject, author (committee), and title, along with detailed abstracts and analyses of the bills and studies. Encapsulated histories of each piece of legislation are provided as well. A large library or one with a government or public affairs specialty is a likely place to look for *CIS/Index.*

Compilations of Federal Laws

United States Statutes at Large contains each year's compilation of laws passed by Congress. Published by the Government Printing Office, you can find it in libraries, law firms, schools of law, and many government reference rooms. It is difficult to use.

If you can do without it, do. A better approach is through *The United States Code,* 1970 ed. (Washington, D.C.: Government Printing Office, 1971), which arranges these same laws by subject, but only once every six years. The most current edition includes all laws in force as of January 1971. Meanwhile, current laws can be successfully approached through combined use of *Congressional Quarterly Almanac* plus annual volumes of *CIS/Index,* or through the privately published *United States Code Congressional and Administrative News* (St. Paul, Minn.: West Publishing Co., 1945 to date). From 1945 through 1951, its correct title was *United States Code Congressional Service.* The *News* is an annual with monthly supplements. It indexes by subject all laws enacted by Congress, as well as proclamations, and Executive Orders. You'll find these volumes in most law libraries.

Rules and regulations (in force and proposed) governing federal agencies are published five times each week in the *Federal Register,* available at $50 per year from the GPO. The information in the *Register* is arranged by Cabinet Department, then by specific agency within the department. It is not easy for a first-time user to figure out the overall arrangement, and so the government offers a book, *The Federal Register, What It Is and How to Use It,* in aid. You can obtain a copy for $3.00 from the GPO. At the end of each year all regulations in effect are compiled into the *Code of Federal Regulations.*

One last reference work in this area is the *Index to Legal Periodicals* (New York: Wilson, 1908 to date), which refers you to explanations and texts of laws as well as articles on court decisions, themselves a highly specialized kind of government publication. As a general rule, though, if you must obtain laws or legal information, you're better off doing so through a lawyer, law student, or an aide in your congressperson's office (who is probably a lawyer or law student).

If you must consult a specific publication but don't require a copy of your own, your public library is worth trying. Official depository libraries are sent copies of selected government publications. Obviously, they don't keep all of them, but many of the ones you'll want will be in a depository library. You can either inquire of libraries in your area or write to the Assistant Public Printer (Superintendent of Documents), Government Printing Office, Washington, D.C. 20402 and ask for a list of depository libraries.

In many instances, however, you'll want to have your own copy of the publication. The very best way to get printed information from the government is to buy it at a Federal Bookstore. It's quick. There are 24 Federal Bookstores in fifteen states and the District of Columbia; they will have basic reference works plus those most frequently requested titles. (Look in your telephone directory under "U.S. Government" to find out if there is one in your city. Or consult the *United States Government Manual* for a list of all Federal Bookstores.) In cases where you know the name of the issuing agency, try to go directly to that agency. As cited earlier, the Government Accounting Office, the National Technical Information Service, Bureau of the Census, and the Consumer Information Center are examples of major outlets for government publications. If you know the title number of the publication you want — and you will have obtained this from either the *Monthly Catalog,* the agency's own selected catalog, or another index or guide — you can call the agency directly and make arrangements for payment and delivery. Several agencies have their own bookstores and publication sales offices, which makes it still easier to do business with them.

It should be clear by now that I've tried to avoid having you go directly to the Government Printing Office for government publications. In many cases, it will be necessary.

Armed with title and stock number, and ideally, the price of a publication, you may have no choice but to write: Superintendent of Documents, U.S. Government Printing Office, Washington, D.C. 20402. And wait.

Still, there is another way. If time is important but money isn't, there are private companies in or near Washington who will obtain the publications for you. They call themselves "document retrieval experts," and their rates vary. Some charge the cost of the document plus postage and shipping, while the overnight specialists add anywhere from $10 to $50 for "instant" delivery. Look in the Washington Yellow Pages under "Information Services" or "Lawyers Services" or, even better, check the membership directory of the Information Industry Association, *Information Sources* (Bethesda, Md.: Information Industry Association, 1978). You'll find a copy in any business library (or you can call the Association directly and ask for a referral).

Then, finally, there are individual researchers and "go-fors" who will do your legwork, usually at rates cheaper than those charged by document retrieval firms. You would do well to find researchers or writers living in the Washington area. There are freelance associations of them and by this point in this book, you should have ideas of your own as to how you could locate such persons. Professional directories and the yellow pages are but two of the routes you must know about by now. Chapter Eight will steer you closer to such persons.

STATE AND LOCAL GOVERNMENT INFORMATION

State and local government information is a highly specialized and complex field. There is no one good index or catalog that does on a state level what the *Monthly Catalog* does for federal documents. The GPO will have some material on aspects of state and local government, so run a check of that source, by subject, first. There is a *Monthly Checklist of State Publications*

INVENTORY SLIP *No Cards*

_____ No inventory card

_____ Check classification

_____ Check cutter number

_____ Check spine

_____ Check book card

_____ Verify accession number

_____ No book card

_____ Repair

_____ Other

(Washington, D.C.: Government Printing Office, 1910 to date), issued by the Library of Congress, but it includes only those documents actually sent to the Library, a miniscule proportion of what the states actually publish. The *Checklist* has an annual subject and author index.

Another selective guide to the field is David W. Parish's *State Government Reference Publications: An Annotated Bibliography* (Littleton, Col.: Libraries Unlimited, 1974). This work covers approximately 800 state documents, plus a bibliography of articles and books on the subject. That is still only a small sampling of what is available from state agencies.

Other bits and pieces of state publications will be included in general indexes such as PAIS, or more selective lists, such as the *Index to Current Urban Documents* (Westport, Conn.: Greenwood Press, 1972 to date). Even so, you are merely skimming the surface.

To obtain an inclusive idea of the kind of information available at the state level, you must first understand how state government is organized. Consult your state's legislative yearbook, manual, or bluebook (the names vary from state to state), which outlines major agency functions and responsibilities. Your local library will have a copy. Another site to reconnoiter, if only by telephone, is the official state library. Most state agencies must file copies of their reports with the state government library, usually located in the state's capital city. Find the library's location, numbers, and descriptions of its collections in the *American Library Directory* if you are unsure as to where or what it is. On the local level, you should begin with the official organization directory of local government, and then check the municipal government library (not to be confused with your local public library).

Apart from official avenues, I think you'll find your best sense of state and local government information will come from the publications of public affairs organizations. The League of Women Voters of the United States issues a yearly catalogue of its publications on federal, state, and local governmental issues and procedures. Copies are available free from the

League at 1730 M Street, N.W., Washington, D.C. 20036. But more importantly, the various state and local chapters of this organization are valuable information resources. League agenda items on the state and local levels often parallel the functions of state and local agencies. If you have a question and don't know which agency to direct it to, a call to the League should be an early step.

The one essential reference book to state government information is *The Book of the States* (Lexington, Ky.: Council of State Governments, 1935 to date), published every two years. The Council is supported by the fifty states and serves as the research bureau for their agencies, and officials. *The Book of the States* contains information on state constitutions, elections, cabinet departments, salaries, personnel, and historical information as well. Chapters are arranged by subject (Education; Transportation, etc.) with tables giving the specific data for each state. The volume costs $21.00 and is available from the Council of State Governments, Iron Works Pike, Lexington, Kentucky 40578. Your library may also have a copy. While you're at this source, ask for the Council's yearly catalogue, *Publications*, which includes periodicals, reference volumes, and reports on many aspects of state government, from zero-base budgeting to criminal justice standards. There is also a retrospective *Index of Council Publications* and a *State Government Research Checklist* that you may want to order.

The National Municipal League (47 East 68th Street, New York, N.Y. 10021) is a nonprofit organization formed to improve state and local government. Its offices house an 11,000 volume library, including collections of state constitutions for the fifty states. The League acts as an information clearinghouse on state and local forms of government, charters, constitutions, apportionment, budgeting and finance policies, and election laws and procedures. One periodical of importance to anyone in the field is the League's *National Civic Review*, which covers new developments in state, county, and local government. The *Review* is published eleven times a year. Write for a detailed booklet listing the League's other publications.

At the local government level, there are fewer inclusive resources than for the states. Your own city government and local League of Women Voters will offer the most relevant publications and information. *The Municipal Yearbook* (Washington, D.C.: International City Management Association, 1934 to date) is one reference work that contains data on U.S. cities, plus lists of officials for cities with populations over 10,000. The *Yearbook* lists additional sources of information on municipal government.

The National League of Cities–United States Conference of Mayors was formed by 15,000 municipalities and individual cities to provide information and solutions on common problems. The federation represents its members before Congress and federal agencies. With a library of 20,000 books and 800 periodicals, and a full-time information and consultation service, this is perhaps the most valuable resource for anyone working on issues of municipal or city government. You can write for the Conference's most recent list of publications (free) at 1620 Eye Street, N.W., Washington, D.C. 20006. The index is arranged by subject, from Aging through Railroad Land Revitalization. Regular periodicals issued by the Conference include: *Urban Affairs Abstracts* (a weekly); *City Weekly; Nation's Cities* (monthly); and the annual *National Municipal Policy.*

See the Appendix, under the subject heading "Government," for further sources of information on state and local government.

INTERNATIONAL AFFAIRS AND GOVERNMENT

The major attempt at having international government is, of course, the United Nations; not surprisingly it is a mine of information on international affairs and the particulars of its member nations. You can write to the U.N.'s Publishing Service, UNIPUB, Inc. (Box 433, Murray Hill Station, New York, N.Y. 10016), and ask for a free catalogue of its publications. Your own library will have some of them. The U.N.'s single most useful reference work is the annual *Statistical Yearbook* (New York: United Nations Department of Economic and Social Affairs, Statistical Office, 1949 to date). The book gives official data, by subject heading, for over 150 areas of the world. Employment, transportation, health, age, education — there are tables and charts on these subjects and more.

If your work or interests are in the field of international affairs, this volume along with the *Statesman's Yearbook* (see p. 31) should be on your permanent reference bookshelf. Be sure to look at the publications list at the end of each section on international organizations in the *Yearbook*. The U.N. also publishes a *Monthly Bulletin of Statistics* and more specialized statistical publications: *Demographic Yearbook; Yearbook of International Trade Statistics;* and *Yearbook of Labor Statistics* are three. The guide to ongoing U.N. activities is the *U.N. Monthly Chronicle,* which has an annual index. But there are thousands more U.N. publications, on subjects large and small, so get the catalogue for future reference. There is one complete but outdated index of U.N. publications which your library might have: Harry N. M. Winton, *Publications of the United Nations System: A Reference Guide* (New York: Bowker, 1972). Although it is old, much of the bibliographic information is still useful.

Other sources of information on foreign affairs are the regularly published world news periodicals. Chief among these is *Facts on File: A Weekly World News Digest, with Cumulative Index* (New York: Facts on File, Inc., 1940 to date), which your public library probably receives. *Facts on File Yearbook,* an annual volume, is perhaps of even greater value; its "World Affairs" and "Other Nations" categories should be checked early in your search process. Your library will have as well the *Europa Yearbook* (London: Europa Publications, 1946 to date), a basic ready-reference source that gives a variety of statistical, educational, cultural, and historical data for all the countries of the world. Appearing annually, the *Yearbook* consists of two volumes: the first covers International Organizations and Europe; the second, Africa, the Americas, Asia, and Australia.

There are many lists and catalogs of the publications of governments other than the United States (*Canadian Government Publications* and the British *Government Publications* are two English-language ones) and just as many standard international yearbooks and handbooks. For a more specialized list, see the subject heading, "Government," in the Appendix.

In general, though, you can always begin with the consulate or embassy of the country about which you seek information. Then, after scanning the U.N. list and some of the works cited here, you can move on to the publications and staffers of foreign policy groups and foreign trade associations. Consult the *Encyclopedia of Associations* in your library, under the section "Public Affairs Organizations" for some good suggestions on whom to call. Schools of International Affairs and librarians at nonprofit foreign libraries (look these up in the *American Library Directory* under your city or state or under the New York City and Washington listings) are other "best" avenues to the information you want.

8

professional researchers

Often, the quickest and best way to get information is not to go after it yourself but to find someone who can do it better and faster than you. Assessing whether and when that is the case is not easy: Money and faith in the person's knowledge and accuracy are two key considerations. Nonetheless, you will find times when you are *not* the best person to do the job; knowing who else is available will help you recognize when that time is at hand.

Except for highly technical research, let me reiterate that if you've read this book and taken some of the advice offered herein, you *are* the best person to get your own information. What you may lack in state-of-the-art knowledge, you make up for by understanding the purpose and "why" of your search. The difference is, of course, the time factor: It may take you too long to learn the ins and outs of available information sources for your project. At such times, you (or your firm) weigh that cost against the cost of using a professional information getter.

DETERMINING THE KIND
OF RESEARCHER YOU NEED

Are you merely after a fact or answers to specific questions? If your search is of the ready-reference nature, you may be able to have it done, for free, and over the telephone by librarians. The more specific your research need, the better your chances are of having it fulfilled quickly and inexpensively. But then if the problem were that specific, you'd probably opt to work on it yourself. The next range of research need falls within what I'll call the odd-job category — you are the one who knows what you need and where it's likely to be found, but you can't get to the source yourself. Document retrievers, picture researchers, (where you know exactly what kind of picture you want), and fact-finders are examples of the "go-fors" you may wish to use, at this level. At the next higher level of searching you want the researcher to have slightly more input — whether it's in selection of material, or choice of sources. You're paying for a thinking individual to hunt for and then organize the information you need. The highest level of information specialist is someone (or a team) who will serve as either a full-time consultant or the real manager of a research project. This function is most often performed by larger firms, which go by various names: management consultants, research and development companies, or other names that round out to "think tanks."

Freelance Researchers

It's difficult to assess what training or background makes for a good professional researcher because the qualities do not seem to parallel any one profession. Persons who have gone to graduate library schools often become independent researchers; and one certainly finds a preponderance of law students doing research for political candidates and office-holders. Picture researchers may have been art history majors in college, amateur photographers, museum or gallery assistants, or none of these; while those in polling and market research may have a strong background in mathematics but nothing else in common. Because there is no one training ground for researchers, they're not easy to locate. Once you do find them, it's not easy to verify their backgrounds and experiences. That means that when you have used someone for research whose work was good, you should keep that person's name, fees, and other particulars in your reference files. Meanwhile, keep the names of any researcher whose work you hear about.

Where you find freelance researchers will to some

extent depend on the field you're in, even if all you want is a "go-for." If you need a federal document retriever obviously you'll look for someone in the Washington, D.C. area; if historical research or fact-checking is called for, you'll be apt to start contacting graduate school history departments and asking for referrals from them. You should always keep in mind that library schools usually have lists of independent researchers, many with experience in using sophisticated computerized research techniques.

Jobs often performed by librarians on a freelance basis include analyzing information, compiling bibliographies, cataloging, verifying facts and/or references; indexing and abstracting, running computer searches, organizing personal and company reference collections; organizing statistics; photocopying; retrieving books, journals, patents, government documents; and finding experts in a field. College and university libraries or schools of library science often keep referral lists of individuals who do these jobs; and their fees are reasonable. A new trend is for such schools and libraries to institute their own for-a-fee research service. Ask both your public library and one at a university near you if it has information services.

Library schools (which are now frequently called Schools of Information Studies and other names without "library" in the titles) also run conferences for people working in the research field. The directories of these conferences usually include the names and addresses of all participants as well as indications of their specialties. Explore this avenue by calling several schools near you, to find out if they have held such meetings and if that kind of material is available.

Another source of competent freelancers is the large number of nationwide or local writers organizations: The Washington Independent Writers Association, The American Society of Journalists and Authors, Inc., The Word Guild — these groups can refer you to someone whom they have screened and whose experience fits your needs. There are also associations of writers and researchers who specialize in particular fields: American Medical Writers Association, Associated

Business Writers of America, Direct Marketing Writers Guild, to name a few. See "Professional Researchers" in the Appendix for a more detailed list.

Independent researchers advertise their services, too. The yellow pages will always reveal a few names under "Writers" or "Information Services." Of more value, however, are the service and resource sections of industry-wide directories. *Literary Market Place* lists only full-fledged firms under its heading "Research and Information Services," but you'll find a large list of persons who actually do research under the headings "Freelance Editorial Work," "Consulting and Editorial Services," and "Photo and Picture Sources." You might consult such directories as the *Madison Avenue Handbook, The Political Marketplace,* or *The Directory of the Direct Marketing Industry.*

At the "go-for" level, what can independent researchers do for you? They can acquire documents or publications from places you can't get to; they can go into government offices or libraries and copy material that can't be taken out; they can prepare bibliographies on a subject; or look through books that you have specified; they can compile data of any kind, with your specifying the sources; or you can merely state your topic and request that they check all relevant periodicals and books. At this level, expect to pay anywhere from $5 to $25 per hour — higher if the researcher must have specialized experience in using the sources to be checked.

Researchers, of course, do more than just retrieve already specified information. Some of the various jobs that a researcher can do are: help you write a book, come up with background ideas for a television program, interview people who are testing your product, find illustrations for a book or brochure, transcribe and organize taped material, chart the movements of publicly traded stocks, write grant proposals for a nonprofit group or agency, write a speech, develop an agenda for an all-day conference, clip newspapers for articles on selected topics, plan a display, scout out competition in a particular industry, run a data base search, verify the credentials or references of a job applicant, or organize a public relations campaign. Although many of these jobs are offered by research firms as part of a total package of what they do for clients, they are often performed by individual researchers, working on either an hourly or fee-per-project basis. Do some research of your own in exploring writer's organizations, directories, and schools in your geographic area and you'll find the researchers who will prove useful to you. And don't think these people are to be found only in large metropolitan areas. I know of several researchers working out of their homes in small towns, hooked up to on-line data base systems, who are used by doctors, lawyers, businesses and government agencies located as far away as 200 miles.

Firms: Specialists in a Field

Also keep in mind those companies who go by names that seem to have little to do with research or information services. They are not, strictly speaking, researchers. Their subject area determines how much research they actually do. You should keep lists of the ones that relate to your work. Market researchers, pollsters, personnel researchers (executive search firms), public relations specialists, editorial consultants, stock research and analysis firms, advertising agencies, historical consultants are a few you've heard of. You find them through word of mouth and the yellow pages, but the primary sources are the directories, handbooks, and associations of their fields. They usually work on a project-fee basis, although they sometimes charge a combination of project-fee plus expenses or fee-plus-hourly charge.

Firms: Information Brokers or Total Research Servicers

These are the ones to know about; they constitute a mushrooming industry that grows bigger each day. Some of these companies are no more than two or three individuals with a particular specialty. The firm of Washington Researchers, now a multimillion dollar research and publishing concern, started out several years ago as one man with a well-thumbed copy of the *United States Government Manual.* He was able to turn that "expertise" into a full-time business whose specialty is "getting information for business out of Washington."

The industry is indeed growing, but it is also an exceedingly volatile line of work. Companies go out of business as new ones enter, and existing ones are constantly trying to determine which kinds of research services will prove the most successful. As a result, one information broker is not just like another, although you may discern that certain distinct types have emerged.

The first type is the research firm that is primarily a publisher of information. This is a lucrative end of the information business, and firms that began with the idea of providing research on demand for clients soon found themselves with a high overhead (staff and materials) that didn't always translate into high profits. Publishing research material, however, especially already existing material which you merely have compiled or reorganized in a new way requires less of an investment; yet there seems to be a willingness, especially on the part of large businesses, to pay high prices for such specialized information. Many of the reference materials cited in Chapters Six and Seven of this book are published by private firms who have taken the time to explore what is out there in the way of information, then organize it along new or more useful lines. Many such works are indeed useful to persons working within that special area or type of source; but many are nothing more than expensive, gussied up versions of information that was available in a very similar form for less money (in many cases for free). The big three reference work publishers are: The H. W. Wilson Company, Gale Research Company, and the R. R. Bowker Company. But they are book publishers, not research firms.

The more typical example of researcher-publisher is a firm like the Washington Service Bureau, which both retrieves government documents, filings, rulings, etc. (you specify subjects or particular documents) for business clients and also issues its own reporting services. These include *Significant SEC Filings Reporter,* the *Supreme Court Brief Service, The Court of Claims Update,* and *Daily Energy Watch,* the latter a service that monitors all rulings and notifications coming from the Department of Energy. Clients also pay a firm like this to monitor activities in government that affect their businesses. See the Appendix, under the heading "Professional Researchers" for a list of selected firms in this line of work.

From that level on down, you move into the field of business publishing, journal publishing, reporting services, and micropublishing. The wares of these firms are described in their brochures or in the entries of those that are listed in the Information Industry Association's *Information Sources,* 1978–79 ed. (Bethesda, Md.: Information Industry Association, 1979). This membership directory includes over one hundred companies in the information field, with entries that give good detail about the kinds of services available. In the back of the book is a convenient index that arranges entrants by types of services provided. You can consult a copy of the book in your library or send for one of your own (for $10 from the Association.

A second type of research firm is one that does information retrieval exclusively. These companies provide the client with information, but not analysis or recommendations. They fulfill the function that a firm's own in-house research department would fill, if it had one. They find experts, interview, locate facts and statistics, do demographic breakdowns of markets, search indexes and abstracting services, and government publications, and usually have on-line access to data bases. A few provide the service of designing reference libraries for businesses. They will tell you which materials you need for your line of work, then obtain them, and organize a system for their classification. All these specialists are usually hired directly by you, the client; although occasionally you might be using them through another kind of research specialist (market research, for example) that you've retained. You hire them on either a retainer basis, by the hour, or by the project. Fifty dollars per hour is an average fee for such service.

The typical research firm, however, is a full-service company, one that specializes in instant-information and special projects. That means that you or your company might pay them on a retainer basis (average, $150 per month) in order to be able to call and say, "Get me this" or "Find out this." That firm would have a large library of its own reference materials, a trained staff of researchers operating at varying levels, from document retrieval to analytic reporting, and probably on-line access to the major data bases as well. Then, on a separate fee basis, you might also use such a firm to handle a special project for you. A client recently hired one of these companies to find information about large-equipment leasing worldwide. The client wished to know how to lease a paper mill in a foreign country: Who does it? What are the economics of the leasing? How do you go about doing it? The researcher assigned to the project was someone who had worked for a large bank's international finance department.

Another client, thinking of entering the golf-cart production business, hired a research firm to provide him with information about the industry — costs, problems, competition, financing — and all trade and tariff laws that pertained to the product. The cost of projects like these will range from $30 per hour, for a simple search, on upward. See the Appendix, under the heading "Professional Researchers" for a list of several of these firms. Then contact them for their brochures and service information.

Firms: Management Consultants
and Think Tanks

Some of the information brokers described previously offer services that compete with those of the management consultants. Yet the latter specialize in analysis and recommendations for action. The information they collect is only done with that purpose in mind, and their researchers are more likely to be business school graduates with business experience than librarians or information specialists. Management consultants are hired by companies (and governments) usually to make studies. The studies can be for acquisitions and mergers, competition in markets, internal management systems, compensation policies — on any subject small or large. The process is one of collecting, organizing, evaluating and analysing, reporting and recommending. The largest of these firms, McKinsey & Company in New York and Arthur D. Little in Cambridge, have huge permanent staffs of specialists within subject divisions (Marketing, Banking, Finance, Real Estate, Electronics, Compensation Studies) plus some general all-around researchers who move back and forth as project assistants. In addition, they will hire special analysts on a project-by-project basis. You'll find a list of these firms in the yellow pages under "Management Consultants." Not all are large, and many concentrate on certain industries or subjects.

At the most esoteric level of research service is the so-called think tank. Usually funded by private and public clients, these analysts make studies of subjects as "small" as the advantages to be had by a municipal fire department's switching to nonliquid water for its hoses, and as "large" as the theoretical outcome of a nuclear war between the United States and the Soviet Union. A good description of what think tanks do, who uses them, and why is in Paul Dickson's *Think Tanks* (New York: Atheneum, 1971). Although somewhat dated, the examples and descriptions are still relevant.

RULES FOR USING PROFESSIONAL RESEARCHERS

Assuming that you've decided to hire a professional research service, you've no doubt first collected material on a number of firms who provide the service you want. You've compared price, references, and specialties, have met with representatives of the firms, and have at last, chosen one to hire. Whether your project is large or small, and the service you've hired is provided by a large firm or merely one individual, you still have additional input into the research process. One doesn't merely farm out one's need in the form of a single-sentence request (unless you're just using the searcher for ready-reference items). You must give the researcher as much information as you have about the query.

First, you should communicate your general request: what information you want and why. What is the purpose of your search, what courses of action are you planning on that will be influenced by the information uncovered? Allowing for an occasional need for secrecy, the more information you can give the professional you've hired, the better (and cheaper) will be the quality of his or her work.

Second, give an idea of the forms in which you expect the information to be presented. The forms may be infeasible, but let the researcher tell you if that is the case and why. Meanwhile, let him or her know what form will be most useful to you. Specify if you want your report to include charts, statistical data, and/or illustrations; be as particular as you can from the start.

Third, provide a history of the project up to this point. What have you done on it? What has anyone else done? Where have you looked? If you can detail sources that have already been culled, you will further increase the researcher's effectiveness. Let him or her know where you've looked and the results, but also include any ideas you or others have for potential sources to explore. Don't assume that because you've hired a professional, it's his or her job to know every resource; if you've thought of one, share the information.

Fourth, provide the names of people on your end of the project who can help, either by giving more details about the project or by consulting on materials or experts. Also, specify materials that you have in-house that might be of use to the researcher.

And, last, make certain at the beginning of your

relationship that you both understand time or cost limits to be set on the job. "Search data bases on this but stop when you've reached $300" or "What kind of a library can you put together for our firm for $5000?" are not only entirely acceptable requests to make of professional researchers but, indeed, are quite common.

9

structuring a search

IMAGING THE INFORMATION: OUTLINING

If it's true that research is a process that involves you, your books, libraries, experts, the telephone, reference works, the computer and perhaps professionals, there must be some sort of glue that holds these parts together and makes from them a whole. The glue is outlining.

Discard the notion that an outline is a perfectly detailed organism (with neat columns of Roman and Arabic numerals, capital and lower-case letters) that you hand in to a teacher preliminary to writing your term paper. That is one kind of outlining, and it often helps you finalize the shape of a report or paper; but by the time you can draw up that outline you probably already have collected your information.

The kind of outlining I'm recommending is done *before* you've amassed your information. In fact, by outlining beforehand — and throughout the information-getting process — you'll be able to determine what information you need to obtain. This is creative outlining, using imagination (and limited knowledge) to bring a shape and order to information or ideas you don't have yet. If you will use the process of outlining, you can find out about anything.

Most things can be outlined. That may sound like an affront to creativity and originality, but it's true. You can outline the books in your home, the contents of your closets, the bills in your "in" basket, the people who work in your company, what you have to do this week, a novel, yes, even a poem or painting. This is not to say that the outline is the entire story of the painting or poem; but it does define and give shape to what otherwise would remain an amorphous "something." There's nothing wrong with some things remaining amorphous, either. One's response to a painting, for instance, need not be outlined. But if you are an art critic, then you must somehow articulate your response in terms that relate to the painting, a body of knowledge about painting, and the human sensibility. Finding and then expressing those terms, I believe, is predicated on having first outlined the response.

Part of what people fear about doing research or getting information about a new subject is that shapelessness of *what is out there.* Not knowing what information there is, they feel paralyzed by the prospect of stepping into the formless nebulae. They don't know where to begin — what is the first "fact" to find — and sense the danger of spending days randomly collecting material, reading, interviewing, only to discover at the end that what they have is an enormous pile of notes that add up to just an enormous pile of notes. Get in the habit of outlining first and you will no longer fear this process.

Outlines should be neither sacred nor immutable. They are experiments at giving shapes to something; experimenting implies "playing with." You must not become too wedded to your outlines or your shape will turn out to have little relationship to its parts. Think of an outline, then, as simply one way of imagining unknown information. There is always another way, perhaps just as good. What makes an outline right for you is whether it enables you to search for and then organize facts and ideas.

Practice playing with outlining as a tool. Start with a simple "something," such as the contents of a closet, say, a man's closet. You might first imagine its form thus:

I. Top shelves

  A. shirts

  B. sweaters

  C. shorts

II. On rod

  A. suits

  B. pants

III. Bottom shelves
    A. shoes
    B. boots
IV. Wall hooks
    A. ties
    B. belts

but then you might reconsider and outline that very same closet this way:

  I. Outdoor clothing
    A. evening
    B. business
    C. casual
    D. active sports
 II. Indoor clothing
    A. evening
    B. business
    C. casual
    D. active sports

Or you might look at that imaginary closet on another day and outline it in terms of winter, spring, and summer garments; or in terms of fibers (wool; blends; silks; cottons, etc.); or in terms of clothes you never wear, clothes you sometimes wear, clothes you wear every day. There are probably three or four more outlines one could make that would "fit" the closet. Keep in mind that you have no concrete knowledge about what is actually in that closet. You are simply imagining the form and parts its contents are apt to take. That's what you should do with any subject you wish to know about, whether it's a closet's contents or a decision to risk capital in a new business venture.

    This is the time to say that the forerunner of an outline is a list; and if you don't yet feel comfortable outlining everything, first practice making lists. List what you must do one week ("make dentist appointment;" "write Aunt Jane;" "finish a book;" "think about ways of earning money;") in any order. Don't worry that your lists are imbalanced, that the items are of unequal weight. Once you get in the habit of listing, you'll find that your lists have assumed new forms: categories and headings will appear, such as "to do at once," "long-term" or "home," "work." You have begun to impose an order on "what you must do" — you have begun an outline.

For a time, apply the process of outlining (make it simple listing, if that's easier) to any subject you need to find out about, either for work or personal use. Here's how one person outlined a subject she had to learn about, and quickly, too.

Lee A. was assistant to a partner in a nationwide accounting firm. Her division serviced retail clients — large department stores throughout the country. Lee was not an accountant. Her job involved developing ancillary services or materials that the firm could offer to its clients or to potential clients. Her boss wanted "something done on profit improvement opportunities for retailers." He saw the need for an attractive but informative book that could be sent to existing and prospective retail clients. Lee's assignment was to research, write, and produce a booklet on that topic.

At the time, though, she had worked in the firm for only six months, and her knowledge of retail operations was slight. She could ask the accountants about the field, but it was not easy to grasp their terminology or slant. Besides, the accountant's point of view was not what was needed. Instead of digging in files and libraries for a basic grounding in her subject — which she didn't have time to do — Lee began by drawing up a list. Her first list itemized whatever areas of retail operations she could think of, off the top of her head. These were no more than simple key words: (1) Buying; (2) Receiving; (3) Pricing; and (4) Selling.

Next, she took each item on the list, in turn, and tried to imagine the parts that would comprise that operation.

Her second list was:

1. Buying

    Ordering (How is it done? How can it be done better?)

    Regular suppliers; new suppliers

    Buying basic items

    Buying specialty items

    Procedures

    Terms of delivery

2. Receiving (How is it done?)

    How do items get moved from receiving room to where customers see them?

    Processing incoming items (checking against the orders; returns for mistakes or damages . . .)

    Moving to selling area (Who moves and how; security?; loss through moving? How long does it take?)

3. Pricing (Who does it and how?)

4. Selling

    a. Sales staff (hiring, paying, conditions, turnover, procedures, training)

    b. Promotion and advertising

        newspaper ads (cost, design, who does?)

        in-store displays (cost, design, who does?)

        promotion of special sales, etc. (cost, design, who does?)

        monitoring ads and displays (cost, design, who does?)

        public relations in the community

    c. Customer services — credit, directories, restrooms, etc.

You'll notice that the list gradually was being transformed into an outline, although many of its parts were vague or incomplete. Lee didn't know at this stage what information was missing, and so the outline was imbalanced. Because of a lack of experience in retail operations from the retailer's side, Lee's most detailed section of the outline was the part that a consumer would be able to imagine, i.e., selling.

However, it didn't matter that the outline at this stage was weighted heavily that way, or that key components were missing, or that items she separated into two categories should really have been one (Lee was to discover that pricing is actually part of the receiving process in a store). She had imagined enough of a form so that she could now go out and fill in blanks and make changes. She had structured her search.

After studying accountants' letters of recommendations to clients, reading articles in the retail trade press and talking to accountants in various departments of her firm, Lee was able to get the information she needed to produce the book. If you were to outline her finished product you would see that it bears very little resemblance to her original scheme. That is as it should be. The point is that she couldn't have reached the final form, couldn't have begun her search even, without that first imagining.

The imagining of an outline was not the very first step, though, of this information search. Key-wording preceded that, but there was an even earlier step, that had been taken by Lee's boss when he said that no one had done a piece like this one before. The proper first step of a search — whether it's for information whose form you know or for information whose form you are still imagining — is to find out if that search has been performed by someone else. Unless the someone else is a direct competitor of yours, that person will be willing to talk to you and share information. You'll save yourself a lot of time, even the time it takes to imagine outlines.

Frank S. was an assistant producer on a television series of twelve shows dramatizing events from American history. For the first show, he had to locate "extras" to play a regiment from the colonial militia. They had to appear in uniforms and with weapons that were historically accurate; and they had to march or stand and shoot the way real soldiers would have fought in 1776.

There were at least three ways to attack Frank's search immediately: One was to do the historical research (or pay to have it done) on uniforms, weapons, commands, and formations and then to instruct the actors as to the proper bearing and positions. Another way was to get in touch with historical groups or organizations — revolutionary war buffs preferably — and ask them for names of colonial soldier-playing troops. A check of the *Encyclopedia of Associations's* index (Revolution; History; American History) or telephone calls to some well-known groups (Daughters of the American Revolution; Sons of the American Revolution) would be sure to result in leads. The third way was simply to ask one's self "Has there ever been a television show (or film, if you have to go that far) that portrayed battle scenes of the American Revolution?" All you then would have to do would be to locate the television station (or film company) that ran the show, call up and get the whereabouts of that producer or assistant producer and talk to that person. You could find out whom they used (or whom they didn't use but found out about). Frank chose that way to find soldiers. Because the United States Bicentennial had occurred, and with it a plethora of television shows and short films made in celebration, he was able to cast a troop of authentic colonial militia within two weeks. One cannot promise that there will always be someone who has done exactly what you're aiming to do, but if there is such a person, you ought to try first to find him or her. Pick their brains before you have to fall back on your own.

As time-saving as such a step can be when you're going after facts or names, it becomes crucial when you're faced with having to find something out in order to make a decision. Decision-making is predicated on having information — in your work it's essential and in your personal life it can surely be helpful. Suppose someone comes to you with an idea for a new business venture for your firm. You listen to the person, ask questions, ask to see any written information or analysis he or she might have prepared. But if it's really a new line of work, you don't even know what it is you don't know about it. The person who wants to sell you on the idea is not the person to guide you either. You have to find someone *who has done it before* or at least someone who has thought about doing it before. Talking with that person may not give you the specific answers you need, but it will help you direct and structure your own search for information.

GETTING THE BROAD OVERVIEW

After you've done steps one and two — asked if someone's done your search before; key-worded and imagined an outline of your information — you must acquire a general understanding of your subject. You can't begin to know what to look for, whom to talk to, and where to go, until you have some idea of the boundaries that commonly define your subject. General understanding also means acquiring sufficient terms — jargon, if you will — and sources so that you can ask the questions that will bring in information.

What you need first is a written "quick study" of your subject, if one can be found. It will be easier for you if there's a book nearby that can fulfill this need. Check your personal library first. If you've taken the suggestions in this book for materials to have on your reference shelf, depending on your profession you may always be able to do your quick studies at home. If not, you must go to a library — public, private, or one at work; it doesn't matter as long as it's one that has a reference section.

You've key-worded your subject already, so you have an idea what general *class* of information it falls under. In the reference room, go to the appropriate shelf for that class — you know now whether the library had Dewey or Library of

Congress classification and what class number or letter includes your subject (see pp. 74-77) — and look through one or more general books in that field. If that proves fruitless, turn to a general encyclopedia. I'd suggest consulting more than one if possible, as I've found that invariably the one that will give you the best overview of your subject — *The World Book Encyclopedia* is a personal favorite for ease of understanding and good pictures — may not be the one that will have a bibliography (*Encylopedia Britannica's* bibliographies, for example, are useful leads).

Another invaluable source for overview is the children's section of a library. It may seem like cheating, but children's nonfiction books (particularly those called "young adult") often provide clear and interesting explanations of very complex subjects. And they're shorter than adult books. Many writers I know who are faced wtih an interview or article to do on a subject they know nothing about, run right to the library's children's branch to see if there's anything on the topic there. Don't you overlook that fund of information either.

The next obvious overview sources to consult are the so-called general-interest periodicals and the *New York Times.* You know by now that you scan the former through the volumes of the *Readers' Guide to Periodical Literature* and the latter through the *New York Times Index.*

Now leave the reference room. If your subject is one about which information lies in books, you want to inspect those books in the field that are shelved together in the stacks. If your subject, for example, is adult education, or some part of that, you would want to look in the 374 section (which is the Dewey number for adult education) or at least in the 370's (which is the general education section). Browse through the tables of contents of the books there, and select for reading those that seem to provide a good general coverage of the subject.

If you're fortunate in knowing someone who can and will give you background information about your subject, then, obviously, you want to talk to that person. In this category should be any friend or associate you can think of, to whom you will not be risking much if you ask "stupid" questions. Or a particularly helpful librarian in a library that specializes on your subject is another source. For other leads you should first acquire some broad knowledge before you approach them.

In consulting general sources, you should use certain techniques. What you're after is the kind of information that will help you structure your search and discover what information you need to know. You want an understanding of your subject at this point but you also want as many specific names as possible — names of *the* books on the topic; names of *the* experts; names of any sources that might be useful.

DEFINING THE DIRECTION

Having acquired general knowledge about your subject, you now should be able to make more outlines, including one that will shape your search more definitely.

First, list sources — known, potential, and unknown. Your list may start out as simple as "Books; Magazines; Experts;" but try to transform it into as much of an outline of specific potential sources as you can:

   I. Books
      A. General library — card catalogue
      B. General library — reference books
      C. Indexes and abstracts
  II. Magazines
      A. General
      B. Of the trade
      C. Special research/special interest
 III. People

IV. Places

    A. Government offices

    B. Special libraries

Write under these and other categories the names of any people, places, books, magazines, etc. that you have already garnered from your general reading and from previous chapters and the Appendix of this book; but also write down "ideas" you have on places to look for — "might there be a museum covering this topic?" "Try calling companies in such-and-such a field," "What nonprint materials (films; slides) are there?" Include any and all long shots for information you have thought of while reading. Keep this outline with you as you work on your project; and update it constantly, filling in specific names whenever they can be filled in. It will serve as a good guide and memory check on where you are in your work.

        As you explore these sources, you will find out that some are worth spending a lot of time on (which will involve detailed notetaking), while others are not. So that you do not retrace your steps, you should enter a separate card to each source to be looked at. Buy 4″-by-6″ index cards for this purpose; even better, buy them in several different colors and use one color for individual printed reference works (books, magazines, abstracts, etc.); one for nonprint works (films, data bases, etc.); one for people (experts, leads to experts, any specific names you have seen mentioned or heard about through your search up to this point), and one for places (libraries, museums, companies, government offices, associations). Note on each card the specific information you have about where to find that source, plus whatever notes you have that will help you use the source later ("Chapter Three worth reading;" "Museum of Broadcasting mobbed on Saturdays, avoid;" "Dr. ____ requires a written request for interview"). And, of course, you note publication date, place, authors' names and all other specific information on any reference work for which you draw up a source card, so that if it should become part of your final bibliography, you'll have it on hand.

Now make another list, a simple list of key words that describe or otherwise relate to your subject. From your general reading and querying, you should have picked up some knowledge of the terms and topics that are covered by your subject. They will eventually become your working subject headings, although right now they may not be in any orderly form. Put them down on paper anyway, don't worry that some will be discarded and others added. The more you can outline now, the more direction you will have given to your search. These headings will also be good places to start from in your exploration of the library's card catalog.

You have drawn up a source list (or outline); and a key-word list (or outline). One more is needed to send you off into the specific digging for information that you will do. For want of a better name, I call this an "Approach List" (or outline).

An approach list may indeed be three separate lists. Faced with an unknown subject, or a mass of information out there which must be mastered, one has to find a slant through which to get at that information. For example, in learning a foreign language, one could drown by endlessly memorizing vocabulary (nouns, verbs, pronouns) in no particular order; but instead if one views that language through the prism of five standard declensions and five conjugations, to which most words apply, plus exceptions, the information becomes more manageable. So it is, with any new information. Find the organizing angle and you've almost structured your search already.

The best approach — if it is at all possible with your particular subject — is a chronologic one: What happened first, what happened next, etc. If you're able to map out a simple chronology of your subject, you can begin filling in the information, even though you haven't actually collected it yet. A chronological approach doesn't merely apply to historical topics, either. Almost any subject has a sequential framework. If you recall Lee A.'s booklet on retail operations, you'll see that key to her understanding was her breaking the "store" down into chronologic terms: Stores must plan what mer-

chandise they will sell; then they order it; then they receive it; then they price it; display it; sell it; take returns; send back unsold items; and so on. That's one kind of chronologic approach to a subject. Later, Lee could fill in the parts of the process that she hadn't been aware of. And you can do that later with your subject, too. But for the present, draw up a simple chronology for your topic, whether it has specific dates or is rather the kind of history-of-events approach that Lee applied to the retail business.

A second way to approach your subject is through the actors involved. Who are the persons key to your subject, not as sources but as principal doers? You wouldn't approach physics, for instance, without taking note of Newton, Galileo, and Einstein. The same is true for other subjects: There are key individuals whose activities may have formed the subject entirely. You can get at the subject by locating those actors. Your actors may not have names, either. Using Lee's retail project once again, this approach would outline buyer, purchasing department, floor manager, checker, salesperson, and other nameless persons as the key actors in her subject. Understand their activities and you can understand retail operations.

Once in a while, the key actors are not even persons or groups of people. If you ever research issues involving government or politics, you discover that laws are often key "actors." Gathering information about the status of capital punishment in America, for instance, can be hinged onto three nonhuman "actors:" the Eighth Amendment to the Constitution and two Supreme Court decisions. You would find that out at once from merely a brief general reading of the subject. If you then go to the original sources and read the Amendment and the two decisions, then collect information on which states were affected by the court rulings and how, and lastly search reactions (pros and cons) to those rulings, you will have not only defined your search but will have actually completed it. What's more, you'd be well on your way to reorganizing your information for presentation.

Your key actors list may closely parallel your

chronologic list. However you should keep the two separate, until you see that that will be the case. Until then, they serve as checks on each other, making certain that you will search for *all* the information relevant to your subject.

A third way of approaching undefined information is by examining all pros and cons of the subject. This will not apply to all topics, certainly, but for those that it does it can be a helpful hook on which to hang information to be gathered. For example, one can approach the subject of capital punishment by finding out what those who are for it have said versus what those against it have said. Again, that approach would help determine not only the information to be collected but the form of the final presentation. It is difficult to see how using this approach would have helped Lee A. define her search into retail operations, but it is not inconceivable that there is some central argument or controversy in the business that she might have used as a springboard into further information. Consider this approach as one possible route for your own research to take.

Although it's true that one should read original documents that apply to one's subject, I'll qualify that to suggest that before you read the original text, read some of what others say about it. Granted, you'll be getting a point of view that will later have to be verified or weighed against the other side's point of view; but I think it's much easier to get at some subjects first through an expert's rendering than to begin with the original, often complex, document. For example, if you try reading the text of a proposed state power commission's request for a rate increase for telephone users, you'll find it difficult to glean information from the wordy, often legalistic provisions. But now instead read testimony at a public hearing on that rate increase. Read both sides: the telephone company's point of view, then that of a consumer group testifying against the increase. You may not be swayed by either, but I suspect you'll be able to derive more information from the original text *after* you've had the pros and cons outlined for you.

With your outline source, key-word, and approach

list (or lists), your work should now be cut out. You have enough subject headings under which to look, enough ideas as to where to look (perhaps still general ideas but now you can narrow them down to specific persons and reference works), and at least one angle from which to consider your subject. Not all of these will work; many headings, actors, and sources will have to be changed or omitted as your searching becomes more detailed. And new ones will be added. In fact, as you delve into your subject further, you may come up with an entirely new slant or subject heading that will define your search and final form better than previous ones. But at least you have structured your search for information. The rest is digging, sifting, and refining.

DIGGING: TAKING NOTES

Digging is simply exploring your information sources: reading, interviewing, and taking notes as you go. Other chapters have outlined procedures to follow in using libraries, checking reference works, and locating and interviewing experts. Those acts are the digging part of a search. The one procedure remaining that helps sift the information that is out there is note-taking. Your notes become your information.

Try to key your notes to both your bibliographic (or source) cards and your subject heading (or key-word) cards. That way you won't have to recopy lengthy citations or phrases. One method of doing this is to select out information as you read (or interview). On your sheet of paper (I suggest paper as preferable to index cards for notetaking as there's more space for changes, comments, and citations) specify the source used in a brief form ("U.S. Govt. Manual"), then write down the subject heading that applies to the particular extract you're reading. If you've worked up a highly detailed outline by this time, you can simply key the extract to the appropriate number or letter on your outline; otherwise simply write fully the appropriate subject heading. Be sure you note any book mentioned in your reading (with a separate bibliographic card for each one). Remember, as you take notes, your outline and its headings may change significantly, becoming more specific or dropping categories that were there at the start. Make those changes on your outline as you go, so that your final notes will relate to that framework.

Much has been written on what one's notes should be: Books on how to write term papers contain entire chapters on the question of whether and when a note should be a direct quote, a paraphrase, or one's own idea about the original text. I think you'll find it a lot simpler to select the material in a source that relates to your topic, then copy it verbatim. Take the book home if you can; if not, try to photocopy the extract at the library; as a last resort, you may have to write it out by hand. Also, always photocopy charts, tables, or illustrations you may want to use. Then, when organizing your material you can either paraphrase or comment on the idea contained in the extract. This way, you will have ruled out the possibility of misquoting or unconsciously plagiarizing. It always pays to have the verbatim account in front of you. When copying quoted extracts, by the way, be sure you have indicated which pages are excerpted and where in the excerpt the page turned. You do this by marking a slash at the appropriate break: An excerpt noted pp. 43–44 "When in the course of human events/it becomes . . ." would thus indicate that "events" was the last word on page 43, and the rest of the quote fell on page 44. If you ever have to request permission to reproduce that excerpt in your book, article, or report, you'll be able to specify the exact pages without having to refer again to the original book.

Separate your notes soon after taking them. If, from one source, you are transcribing information that will go under more than one heading in your outline, separate them now. Either copy each extract on a separate sheet of paper, specifying source again on each; or cut apart your notes after you've transcribed and specify the source and subject heading on each half of the page. In the case of an interview transcript, this separating is essential, because certain parts of the interview will touch on differing aspects of your outline. As I said earlier, *always have two copies made of an interview transcript.* One will be for cutting and pasting along the lines of your final outline; the other you will need to retain intact for verification purposes.

The last rule of notetaking is to verify sources that you use as you go along. Notice whether a book is new, a new edition, or merely a new reprint of an old edition. This can be a crucial factor in its reliability, particularly if your topic is in a scientific or technologic field, where information is fast superseded by newer information. Another means of verification is to consult reviews of books you use. A check of *Book Review Digest* (see p. 108) is always a good idea. Biographical reference works will help you verify the backgrounds and credentials of authorities whose work you plan to cite. Common sense and a willingness to ask others (librarians or experts) are the other ways by which you verify whether a source you're using is accurate, slanted, responsible, or ill-valued by those in the field. Verification is the final step in determining whether the information you imagined does indeed exist and how you can shape it to fit your needs.

10

reorganizing and presenting information

What was the purpose of your research? Why did you take the time to find out about a subject? In what form are you to disclose what you found out? You must continue to ask yourself these questions as you structure your search, collect information, and now, especially, as you prepare to present the result of your work. This book can outline several general rules to follow in reorganizing your material and writing it for presentation, but it cannot take into account the vagaries of purposes and audience that in the end must dictate your final research product. If your assignment, for instance, was to respond on behalf of your firm to a proposed rules change by the Securities and Exchange Commission, then the procedures you follow from this point on will be very different from those used by the researcher whose job was to do a study of rates charged for all services by outpatient health clinics in Chicago. The general rules that follow, then, are guidelines, not necessarily ones that will work for your project.

MAKING A FINAL OUTLINE

No matter what form your product will take, you should now be able to draw up a detailed outline. This outline is like the one I spoke of earlier, the one you might have handed in to a teacher who then gave the go-ahead to you to write up a term paper. The particulars of this outline will depend on your project, but the basic components of it are: Theme; Background and Approach; Ideas and Analysis; and Conclusions or Recommendations.

A theme statement may be a simple definition of what you set out to find transformed into a declarative sen-

187

tence. "There are many ways by which retailers can improve their profit-making opportunities" or "We should do our next show in the series on the Battle of Gettysburg" are theme statements.

"Background" is where you reveal your approach, the perspective through which you will view the material amassed. It is here that you provide basic information that will facilitate a reader's (or listener's) understanding of the topic. "Ideas and Analysis" detail the particulars of your research; they may be your points; your responses to points made by others; facts strung together in a particular sequence, or various other configurations of the specifics of your research. Your own ideas should form the major part of this section. Those ideas need not have originated with you, but you must here restate, consider, and "answer" them on your terms.

The last section contains your summarization(s), conclusion(s), and recommendation(s), if these apply to your topic. The information you've given in earlier sections of your report presumably lends credence to the views you take here. In writing this section, you must link that information to the final conclusion, show how the one leads to the other.

Before you proceed to fill in that outline, or one very much like it, consider these steps where they apply to your project:

When the point of your work was to answer the question: "What should we (I) do?" you should write that answer right now on a sheet of paper. The specific question might have been "Should our firm be for or against this legislation?" "Should we change the way we bill clients?" "Should I write an article on sheepdogs?" or any other question that posits a course of action to be taken. Before you outline what you found in detail, you want to have your answer in front of you: "The bill ought not to become law," "I should write an article on sheepdogs," etc. The rest of your presentation, whether it's to be a letter, memo, speech, or lengthy paper, will be the "Why" of this statement. The "Background" section of a "what-to-do project" outline would define terms and perhaps give a chronological approach — anything that would prepare the reader for an understanding of your later arguments. In the case of responding to legislation, for example, background would include an explanation of the meaning of the bill, who introduced it, its history and the history of events that led up to its proposal. Analysis and Ideas would consist of responses of others to the legislation, outlining the "sides," plus your own analysis and/or critique of others' analyses. The concluding section might then be merely a restatement of your beginning "what we should do," or it might detail the "how" of what you (or someone else) should do, with concrete proposals and anticipated results or reactions.

Even in cases in which research was done *not* for the purpose of suggesting a course of action but simply to gather information, I suggest you try to imagine an intended purpose as you order your material for presentation. The chances are that someone had a purpose in mind, but either wasn't certain about how to articulate it or didn't want to divulge the purpose. For example, the person asked to find out rates charged for health services by private and nonprofit outpatient clinics in Chicago, was never told the purpose of the report, and in fact a third party had hired him to do the research. The researcher imagined, however, that the firm wanting the information was considering entering the field and would therefore want to know the size and details of the competition. All along the steps of his search he would ask himself, "What would I want to know if I were considering going into this business?" In the presentation he could not presume to begin his report "There is room for new entrants in the outpatient health care field" or anything similar to that. But he could order his material so as to begin with several clear definitive statements about the industry in general, then proceed to background and particularize its features. He had not been asked for conclusions or recommendations so there were none in the final report and no need for that section in the outline.

Depending on the size and scope of your subject,

the four sections of your outline may be reduced to three, or even two; the sections may have many subsections to them, or only a few; or the parts of your outline might be reordered. Your final report might combine "Ideas and Analysis" with "Conclusions," so that you take up, analyze, and accept or dismiss each point in turn. A letter or speech is often well suited to such combination, as your purpose is to briefly and forcefully convince someone of a point of view. Even longer projects may use this approach effectively. Lee A.'s final product for retail clients was a questionnaire in glossy booklet form. Each section covered one phase of retail operations and within each section points were raised, detailed, and debated in the same paragraph. That approach enabled clients to turn to the appropriate section and find all the relevant information there instead of having to read through the entire book to find the conclusions at the end. In fact, it's usually only in a long term paper, scholarly research report, or issue paper that one leaves all conclusions until the end.

Until you've become experienced at making outlines, yours will be easier to write from if you make each entry into a statement or complete sentence.

Now that you're ready to do your outline you need only recall that standard outline form consists of Roman numerals for your first subject headings; followed by capital letters for subsections, followed by Arabic numerals for subsubsections; followed by lower case letters. You will rarely need to detail beyond that point, but, if you should, you can proceed to use Roman numerals within a parenthesis, then capital letters within a parenthesis and so on, in sequence. A diagram of an empty outline might look like this

I.

  A.

  B.

    1.

    2.

C.

    1.

    2.

      a.

      b.

    3.

II.

  A.

One last step you may wish to take before doing a final outline of your project is to practice outlining someone else's finished product. Select a short article from any magazine or newspaper and try to outline it, either roughly or in great detail. You will be doing the reverse of the process followed by the writer of the article (or the process that should have been followed), but the practice is valuable for learning to outline in correct order.

A sample outline of this chapter up to this point might look like this

  I. Reorganizing and Presenting Information

    A. Reorganize your information with your purpose in mind

      1. Examples

    B. Make a Final Outline

      1. Defined generally

        a. Theme (explained and exampled)

        b. Background and Approach (explained and exampled)

        c. Ideas and Analysis (explained and exampled)

        d. Conclusions-Recommendations (explained and exampled)

2. Particular considerations and exceptions
   a. When you're recommending course of action (example)
   b. Combining Ideas and Analysis with Conclusions (example)
   c. Imagining a course of action so as to organize material better; but no conclusion (example)
3. Standard form for outlining
4. Practice outlining
   a. Sample outline shown

Now, look at *your* last working outline. (See Chapter Nine for a discussion of working outlines.) Do its categories still make sense to you in terms of what you now know about your subject. If so, you may simply adopt that outline as your final one. If not, you'll want to make whatever alterations are dictated by your information and ideas about the topic.

Read through your notes. Some of them will already be keyed to sections of your last working outline. Other notes may not yet have found a home in the outline. Determine whether each note contains information you want to include in your final product; if so, assign an appropriate heading or category for it to fall under.

Discard notes that now seem irrelevant to your final subject or line of reasoning. But don't throw out information merely because it contradicts the line you're going to take. Your final product will be better if it shows that you have considered opposing views and exceptions to rules you have stated.

Cutting and Pasting

Making sure that the source of each note is specified alongside the note itself, now cut up your notes and place them with the other notes that go into that same section or subsection in your outline. Read through the transcripts of any interviews you've conducted, and key each section to the appropriate number and letter of your outline. Remember to have a copy of the entire transcript made first; you don't want to run the risk of quoting someone out of context or forgetting where in the interview a point was made. After you've keyed all useful parts, discard the others. Again, note a code word for the source on each extract ("Pauling interv." or something short will do — remember, you have a complete source citation for the interview on a bibliographic card). Then cut up the interview into sections and arrange these with your other notes, section by section.

When all your notes and comments have been arranged by outline heading, read through them, one section at a time. Try to put them in an order that will resemble how you want to treat the points in your final presentation. If you can't do that for the entire paper at this point, wait a bit and try taking each section one at a time, as you sit down and actually write it.

FORMS FOR WRITING:
FOOTNOTES AND BIBLIOGRAPHY

Entire books have been written on the subject of the proper forms to use in writing reports or papers. As you begin to write up research on any subject you should have at your side a copy of at least one reference work in the field. *Manual of Style*, 12th ed. (Chicago: The University of Chicago Press, 1969) and William Strunk Jr. and E. B. White, *The Elements of Style*, 3rd ed. (New York: Macmillan Publishing Co., 1979) are two excellent ones. In addition to, or in place of those works, you might buy a style book that relates specifically to research products. Kate L. Turabian's *A Manual for Writers of Term Papers, Theses, and Dissertations*, 4th ed. rev. (Chicago: University of Chicago Press, 1973) is one of the best available in paperback. See the Appendix under the heading "For Writers" for names of others.

Most of the information on forms of presentation that will concern you in everyday research and writing will focus on footnotes and bibliography.

Footnotes are used to explain material occurring in the text of your report, to cite related facts or points of view from other sources, and chiefly to attribute to a source information you've used in the text above. You may list all your footnotes in order at the end of a report or paper; at the end of a chapter or segment of a paper; or at the bottom of the page on which the excerpt falls. The latter is preferable, as the reader can verify then and there where the information came from, and then move on to the next page in sequence. Rustling back and forth from back of book to front, or from end of chapter to middle, does not make for sustained concentration on the part of the reader. Since much of your research will be aimed at convincing or recommending something to someone, you want the reader's complete attention.

If your footnotes are at page bottoms, you either number from 1. on for each page that has footnotes, or you number consecutively throughout the entire paper. If your paper is to have many footnotes, you'd be better off with the former method.

The general form to follow in writing a footnote *when the source is cited for the first time* in a report is: Author's name (first name, then last); Title of Book or publication; then, in parentheses, the place of publication, name of publisher and date of publication; and last, outside the parentheses, the page number(s) your excerpt is from. A complete footnote of this type would be

[1] Thomas Wolfe, *The Story of a Novel* (New York: Charles Scribner's Sons, 1936), p. 15.

If you cite the same source again, with no intervening reference, you would then connote:

[2] *Ibid.,* (which means "the same as the reference immediately preceding it").

If the second footnote cited the same source but the material quoted was on a different page of that source, the proper form would be:

[2] *Ibid.*, p. 17.

If you cite the same source again later on in your report but with intervening references to other sources, a proper citation would be:

[1] Wolfe, *Story of a Novel*, p. 19.

Sample citations for magazine articles, books written by two or more authors, works that have more than one volume or edition, and other common exceptions follow:

[1] J. P. Cooper, "The Fortune of Thomas Wentworth, Earl of Strafford," *Economic History Review*, 2nd Ser., XI (December 1958): 227–248. [author's name, title of article, title of periodical, series and/or volume number of periodical, its date, and pages cited]

[1] Calvin D. Linton, ed., *The American Almanac* (Nashville, Tenn. and New York: Thomas Nelson Inc., Publishers, 1977), p. 105 [where there is an editor instead of author]

[1] William Strunk Jr. and E. B. White, *The Elements of Style*, 3rd ed. (New York: Macmillan Publishing Co., Inc. 1979), p. 13 [where there are two authors; where there is a specific edition cited]

[1] Washington Researchers, *Researcher's Guide to Washington*, 1979 ed. (Washington, D.C.: Washington Researchers, 1979), p. 215. [where the author is an organization or institution]

[1] "Duke, Kaline Voted to Hall," *New York Post*, 9 January 1980, p. 64. [where the reference is to a newspaper article]

A bibliography includes every source cited in your paper plus others that were central to your research. You need not include works you scanned but did not use. The purpose of a bibliography is to give complete information about sources. Bibliographies are arranged in alphabetical order, by authors' last names. Standard bibliographic form is:

> Wolfe, Thomas. *The Story of a Novel.* New York: Charles Scribner's Sons, 1936.

Note that the parenthesis used in the footnote form has disappeared and no page numbers are given. The only exception to this would be if you had used only one section or chapter of a book for reference, in which case you would cite the chapter used. For more than one work by the same author, you omit the author's name in the second reference and insert a line about one-half inch long in its place:

> Wolfe, Thomas. *The Story of a Novel.* etc.
>
> ———. The Web and the Rock. etc.

Usually, all works used — whether they be books, magazine articles, reports or speeches — are alphabetized by authors' names into one complete bibliography. Occasionally, however, someone may prefer to separate books from reports or print materials from nonprint sources or other special designated classifications. If your final product is to be other than a published book or scholarly paper, you may choose such variations. In all cases, though, you should consult a work such as Turabian's to be sure of correct style and forms.

WRITING UP YOUR RESEARCH

With your dictionary and style guide nearby, and your outline and notes in front of you, proceed to write up the results of your research. Take your outline, one section at a time, organize your material (if you haven't already done so for the entire project) and "deliver" your information, to your intended (or imagined) reader. Be brutal in weeding out information. It may be difficult to part with material you spent hours copying, thinking about, cutting and pasting; but if it doesn't further your schematic framework and its presentation, get rid of it.

Unless yours is a particularly open-ended project — say a term paper on a large subject — you should not attempt to include every shred of information that in any way touches upon your topic. Don't try to impress your reader with how much material you have amassed or the extent of your digging. It will be the organization of your material that impresses or doesn't. Also, avoid feeling compelled to produce a perfect no-holes argument. You need not reconcile all information. If there are exceptions to a general rule or argument you are stating, you can simply note the exceptions; explain them if you can, guess at them if you wish, but if you can't explain them away, just let them stand. Your presentation will be better for your having noted opposing points of view where such exist.

I can't advise you on how to write a good final product. If you've organized your material tightly enough you have handled it many times, which means you should be familiar with what information you have and what you think about it. As you write — and I think this should apply to any kind of writing — remove yourself from the process. Forget that *you* did the search, the organization. That's over. Imagine that the information exists, now in a decidedly prepackaged and lucid form; and your job is to find the words to make that package apparent and meaningful to one individual reader.

After you have finished a first draft of your final product, lay it aside, at least for an hour or two (overnight is best). Do something else, then return to your paper. Be the reader for whom you wrote it, and read it from that perspective. Forget all the information you knew as researcher; read it as if for the first time. If there's missing information, a question that comes to mind but isn't dealt with in the paper, make a note to find that additional information. If some sections seem overly long or filled with too many facts that get in the way of a clear presentation, cut them down. And finally, don't feel so wedded to your original arrangement of the material that you can't reorder it if necessary. Information is not unlike the juggler's rubber balls: They have definite forms and colors of their own, but they are without effect until someone comes along and arranges them into large, exciting patterns.

appendix

the searcher's bookshelf

ADVERTISING AND PUBLIC RELATIONS

All-In-One Directory (New Paltz, N.Y.: Gebbie Press). Annual. Lists over 20,000 outlets in all media for public relations.

Ayer Glossary of Advertising and Related Terms, rev. ed. (Philadelphia: Ayer Press, 1977).

Ayer Public Relations and Publicity Style Book, rev. ed. (Philadelphia: Ayer Press, 1977). Names and addresses of feature editors on newspapers with circulation over 100,000.

Gebbie House Magazine Directory (Sioux City, Iowa: Gebbie Press). Biennial. Guide to company house organs; gives information of interest to public relations agents, writers, and artists.

Hansen, Harold (ed.), *TV Publicity Outlets — Nationwide* (Washington Depot, Conn.: Public Relations Plus, Inc.). Annual. Guide to 2,000 T.V. programs that use publicity material or guests; lists requirements and other information.

Hodgson, Richard, *Direct Mail and Mail Order Handbook* (Chicago: Dartnell Corp., 1974). Directory of the business; lists services, suppliers, etc.

National Register Publishing Company, *Standard Directory of Advertisers: Classified Edition;* and *Standard Directory of Advertisers: Geographical Edition* (Skokie, Ill. National Register, 1979). Tells who advertises and for which products. Basic to the industry.

Norton, Alice (ed.), *Public Relations Information Sources* (Detroit: Gale, 1970).

O'Dwyer's Directory of Corporate Communications (New York: J. R. O'Dwyer Co., Inc.). Annual. Lists in-house public relations staffs for U.S. corporations.

O'Dwyer's Directory of Public Relations Firms (New York: J. R. O'Dwyer Co., Inc.). Annual. Lists by client name, type of firm, and city.

Smith, Brian J. (ed.), *Madison Avenue Handbook,* 20th ed. (New York: Peter Glenn, 1977). Annual directory of the industry; lists agencies, services, and suppliers.

Data Bases

(AMI) Advertising and Marketing Intelligence (New York: New York Times Information Service). Stores facts from 60 trade and professional journals, magazines, etc., covering all aspects of the field — new products, industry changes, ad campaigns, expenditures, consumer trends, personnel changes, etc.

ART, ARCHITECTURE, AND DESIGN

American Architects Directory, 3rd ed. Sponsored by the American Institute of Architects (New York: Bowker, 1970).

American Federation of Arts, *American Art Directory,* 47th ed. (New York: Bowker, 1952 to date). Triennial. Includes information on museums, publications, associations, and other sources.

ARTbibliographies Modern (Santa Barbara, Cal.: American Bibliographical Center–Clio Press, 1974 to date). Abstracts of literature in art history, biography, and types of art media; refers to periodicals, books, dissertations, and catalogs. Also on Data Base.

Art Books in Print, 1950–1979, 1st ed. (New York: Bowker, 1979). Bibliography.

1980 Artist's Market (Cincinnati, Ohio: Writer's Digest, 1979). Outlets for the artist, photographer, illustrator; suppliers and services; some information sources listed.

Barton, Lucy, *Historic Costume for the Stage* (Boston: Baker, 1961). Includes directions for making costumes; illustrated history, 4,000 B.C. to 1914.

Carrick, Neville, *How to Find Out About the Arts: A Guide to Sources of Information* (Oxford, England: Pergamon Press, 1965). Still valuable; how to use various kinds of reference books.

Chamberlin, Mary W., *Guide to Art Reference Books* (Chicago: American Library Association, 1959). Long, annotated bibliography of 2,500 books in all fields of art; includes magazines, catalogs, and documents.

Contemporary Crafts Market Place (New York: Bowker). Biennial. Handbook and guide to sources, services, outlets; includes list of books and periodicals in the field.

Directory of World Museums, The (New York: Columbia University Press, 1975).

Ehresmann, Donald L., *Applied and Decorative Arts: A Bibliographic Guide to Basic Reference Works, Histories, and Handbooks* (Littleton, Col.: Libraries Unlimited, 1977). List of works, published 1875–1975, on decorative arts — furniture, toys, folk art, ornament, etc.

——, *Fine Arts: A Bibliographic Guide to Basic Reference Works, Histories, and Handbooks,* 2nd ed. (Littleton, Col.: Libraries Unlimited, 1979). Adds to the Chamberlin work above; covers 1,200 books, arranged by geographic region.

Encyclopedia of World Art (New York: McGraw-Hill, 1959–1968), 15 volumes. Top of the line; covers all periods and subjects; illustrated; includes bibliographies. Most medium-sized libraries and certainly art reference libraries will have this beauty.

Fine Arts Market Place (New York: Bowker, 1973 to date). Biennial. Handbook of information on outlets, sources for information, suppliers, and services.

Focal Encyclopedia of Photography, The, rev. ed. (New York: McGraw-Hill, 1969). Worth looking at, even if you're a beginner; covers techniques, terminology, and sources for information.

Harris, Cyril M. (ed.), *Dictionary of Architecture and Construction* (New York: McGraw-Hill, 1975). Good for the nonspecialist; defines terms and identifies materials.

Havlice, Patricia P., *Index to Artistic Biography* (Metuchen, N.J.: Scarecrow, 1973). Biographical sources for over 70,000 artists.

Jones, Lois S., *Art Research Methods and Resources: A Guide to Finding Art Information* (Dubuque, Iowa: Kendall-Hunt, 1978). Useful paperback edition.

McGraw-Hill Dictionary of Art (New York: McGraw-Hill, 1969), 5 volumes. The other "best work" in the field; illustrated; includes biographies; all styles, periods, and movements.

Photography Market Place (New York: Bowker). Biennial. Handbook of services and suppliers, sources for information, etc.

Richards, J. M. (ed.), *Who's Who in Architecture from 1400 to the Present* (New York: Holt, Rinehart, 1977). With illustrations.

Savage, George, *The Dictionary of Antiques* (New York: Praeger, 1970). Helps identify antiques (and fakes); includes biographical and bibliographical information.

Smith, Denison L., *How to Find Out in Architecture and Building: A Guide to Sources of Information* (Oxford, England: Pergamon, 1967). Bibliographical, primarily British, sources.

Who's Who in American Art, edited by the Jaques Cattell Press (New York: Bowker, 1937 to date). Biographies of living artists, plus collectors, patrons, scholars and art writers; over 9,000 entries, many with bibliographies. Index by subject and geographical region. Available in most libraries.

BUSINESS, ECONOMICS, AND FINANCE

Note: The "field" includes thousands of specialties and subspecialties and entire books have been written on sources for information within only one subspecialty. The following outline the more general reference works available and some of the directories or handbooks essential to anyone in any kind of business enterprise.

Brownstone, David, and Carruth, Gorton, *Where to Find Business Information: A Worldwide Guide for Everyone Who Needs the Answers to Business Questions* (New York: Wiley, 1979).

Business Books In Print (New York: Bowker) Annual. The standard work. Look up your kind of business (or specialty) and see what works are currently available and for how much.

Business Periodicals Index (New York: Wilson, 1958 to date). The best-known subject index; covers 300 periodicals; monthly, except August, with annual cumulations.

Crowley, Ellen T. (ed.), *Trade Names Dictionary* (Detroit: Gale, 1976), 2 volumes. Lists 100,000 trade and brand names.

Daniells, Lorna M., *Business Information Sources* (Berkeley, Cal.: University of California Press, 1976). A first-rate annotated listing of basics and specialized types of business materials. A good start for any search.

Dun and Bradstreet, *Million Dollar Directory* (New York: Dun and Bradstreet). Annual. Essential directory; basic information on 39,000 U.S. corporations worth over $1 million; indexed by industry and geographic area. For firms worth between $500,000 and $1 million, see *Middle Market Directory,* from the same publisher.

Encyclopedia of Business Information Sources, compiled by Paul Wasserman, 4th rev. ed. (Detroit: Gale, 1980). Contains 17,000 entries, by subjects (unemployment, packaging, sales promotion, etc.); includes print and person sources of information. A basic library research tool in business.

Funk and Scott Index of Corporations and Industries (F & S) (Cleveland, Ohio: Predicasts, Inc.). Weekly, with monthly and annual cumulations. The basic book for up-to-date information on companies and industries; Also on Data Base.

McGraw-Hill Dictionary of Modern Economics: A Handbook of Terms and Organizations, The, 2nd ed. (New York: McGraw-Hill, 1973). Useful for layperson; includes bibliographies.

Munn, Clenn G., *Encyclopedia of Banking and Finance,* 7th ed., revised and enlarged by F. L. Garcia (Boston: Bankers Publishing Co., 1973).

Schultz, George J. (ed.), *Foreign Trade Marketplace* (Detroit: Gale, 1977). Handbook of 5,000 companies, consultants, and organizations, arranged by subject and geographic area.

Standard & Poor's Register of Corporations, Directors and Executives (New York: Standard & Poor Corp.). Annual. Another standard directory; gives officers, line of business, sales and employee figures for over 36,000 U.S. corporations; biographical information on executives; indexed.

Washington Researchers, *Washington Information Workbook 1979 Edition* (Washington: Washington Researchers, 1979). Not inexpensive, but a valuable work on how to get business information in the federal government; gives names, telephone numbers, kinds of help you can get within each agency. You may be able to borrow the volume from a Business Library (public or private).

Wasserman, Paul and Bernero, Jacqueline (eds.), *Statistics Sources*, 5th ed. (Detroit: Gale, 1977). Excellent bibliographical source; material arranged by subject heading.

Who's Who in Finance and Industry (Chicago: Marquis Who's Who, Inc., 1936 to date) Biennial. Contains 25,000 entries.

Data Bases

ABI/INFORM (Date Courier Inc.). Scans 400 publications in field of management and administration for article abstracts.

DISCLOSURE. Stores reports filed with the Securities and Exchange Commission by publicly held U.S. corporations.

EIS INDUSTRIAL PLANTS: EIS NONMANUFACTURING ESTABLISHMENTS (Economic Information Systems, Inc.). Two similar bases, storing information on plant location, annual sales, market share, etc.

F & S INDEXES (Predicasts, Inc.). Stores information described in entry above.

FOREIGN TRADERS INDEX (U.S. Department of Commerce). Lists manufacturers, distributors, wholesalers, retailers, and other firms in 130 countries.

PTS PROMT (Predicasts Inc.). Abstracts wide range of newspapers, government reports and business periodicals.

See Also: Wall Street Journal Index; New York Times Index; New York Times Information Bank; Libraries of Graduate Business schools; Trade and Professional Associations (check the *Encyclopedia of Associations* for these).

Berliner, Stan, and Serbell, Carl (eds.), *Consultant's Network* (New York: Consultant's Network). Annual. Directory of specialists in all phases of education; includes list of organizations.

Current Index to Journals in Education (New York: Macmillan Information, 1969 to date). Monthly with semi-annual cumulations; indexes 700 journals; gives full bibliographic information; Also part of ERIC Data Base.

Deighton, Lee C. (ed.), *The Encyclopedia of Education* (New York: Macmillan, 1971), 10 volumes. The big one in the field; covers history, theory, philosophy, and structure of education. You'll find it in a large public library or one connected with a graduate school of education.

Education Index, The (New York: Wilson, 1929 to date). Monthly except June and August. Indexes, by subject and author, the contents of 220 publications.

Good, Carter V. (ed.), *Dictionary of Education,* 3rd ed. (New York: McGraw-Hill, 1973). Defines over 30,000 terms.

Leaders in Education, 5th ed. compiled by the Jaques Cattell Press (New York: Bowker, 1974). Biographical information on 14,000 American and Canadian educators.

Requirements for Certification of Teachers, Counselors, Librarians, and Administrators for Elementary Schools, Secondary Schools, Junior Colleges (Chicago: The University of Chicago Press, 1935 to date). Annual volume that should be consulted by anyone planning to teach or looking for a new position; arranged by state, gives information on positions at all levels.

Resources in Education (Washington, D.C.: U.S. Department of Health, Education and Welfare, National Institute of Education, 1967 to date). A nationwide information storage clearinghouse in education; monthly abstracts of all literature in the field. Also on ERIC Data Base.

Woodbury, Marda, *A Guide to Sources of Educational Information* (Washington, D.C.: Information Resources Press, 1976).

World of Learning, The (London: Europa Publications, 1947 to date). Annual directory of organizations in education; arranged alphabetically, by country.

Data Bases

ERIC (Educational Research Information Center). The all-inclusive data base in the field. ERIC contains all abstracts from *Resources in Education* (see page 115) plus *Current Index to Journals in Education.* Information stored goes back to 1966.

EXCEPTIONAL CHILD EDUCATION ABSTRACTS. Abstracts journals and other material on all aspects of handicapped and gifted children.

GOVERNMENT, LAW, POLITICS, SOCIAL SCIENCES

Note: See Chapter Seven for a detailed analysis of government sources of information.

Black's Law Dictionary, 4th ed., rev. (New York: Scribner's, 1976). This standard work defines terms and concepts, rules for the bar, code of ethics, etc.

Brock, Clifton, *The Literature of Political Science* (New York: Bowker, 1969). Old but still helpful work showing how to use types of reference works and where to find them.

Foundation Directory, The, 5th ed., compiled by the Foundation Center (New York: Foundation Center, 1975). Lists 2,500 foundations with assets over $1 million, arranged by state; indexed to name and field of interest.

Freides, Thelma, *Literature and Bibliography of the Social Sciences* (Los Angeles: Melville, 1973). Arranged by type of material (dictionaries, guides, etc.) with name/title and subject indexes.

Gager, Nancy (ed.), *Women's Rights Almanac* (Bethesda, Maryland: Elizabeth Cady Stanton Publishing Co., 1974 to date). An inexpensive paperback annual on status of women's rights movement; gives statistics, information on elected officials, issues, laws.

The Gallup Opinion Index: Political, Social and Economic Trends (Princeton: The American Institute of Public Opinion, 1965 to date). Monthly reports on survey results. You can also contact the Institute to obtain a copy of the results of any poll on any subject. Call first to see if one's been done on your subject (609-924-9600).

International Encyclopedia of the Social Sciences (New York: Macmillan, 1968), 17 volumes. Theory, methodology — the works; includes some biographical information.

Klein, Barry (ed.), *Reference Encyclopedia of the American Indian,* 3rd ed. (Rye, New York: Todd Publications, 1978), 2 volumes. Sources for information plus biographical information.

Ploski, Harry A., and Marr, Warren (eds.), *The Negro Almanac: A Reference Work on the Afro American,* 3rd rev. ed. (New York: The Bellwether Co., 1976). Historical and biographical; sources for information and assistance.

Rosenbloom, David L. (ed.), *The Political Marketplace* (New York: Arno, 1972). All services, suppliers, and specialists having anything to do with political campaigns.

Shain, Henry, *Legal First Aid* (New York: Funk & Wagnalls, 1975). Good for the general reader; charts show state-by-state summary of laws governing marriage, divorce, civil suits, etc.

Social Sciences Index (SSI) (New York: Wilson, 1974 to date). Quarterly and annual cumulations. Subject and author index to articles in 250 publications.

Theodorson, George A., and Achilles, G., *A Modern Dictionary of Sociology* (New York: Crowell, 1969).

Washington Information Directory (Washington: Congressional Quarterly, Inc.). Annual. Names, numbers and job descriptions of 5,000 persons in government and private agencies, indexed by subject area.

White, Carl M., *et al.* (eds.), *Sources of Information in the Social Sciences: A Guide to the Literature,* 2nd ed., (Chicago: American Library Association, 1973).

Who's Who Among Black Americans (Northbrook, Ill: Who's Who Among Black Americans, Inc., 1976). Contains 10,000 entries.

Who's Who in American Politics, 6th ed. (New York: Bowker, 1977). Covers national, state, and local levels; with geographic index.

Women's Movement Media: A Source Guide, (New York: Bowker, 1975). Directory of organizations, publications, activities.

Data Bases

ASI (American Statistics Index). Stores information from U.S. Government periodicals, surveys, reports, Jan. 1973 to date.

CIS INDEX. Prepared by Congressional Information Service; by-subject storage of U.S. Congress publications, Jan., 1970 to date.

FEDERAL INDEX. Citations to *Congressional Record, Federal Register, United States Code,* and other federal documents, 1976 on.

GRANTS. Contains 1500 programs offered by government, associations, and foundations in 88 disciplines in the sciences and humanities.

LEXIS. Information on federal and state cases, codes, rules and regulations, and decisions of government agencies.

NEW YORK TIMES INFORMATION BANK. Selected material from the *New York Times* and 70 other newspapers and periodicals, many of them in the business fields, 1969 to date.

SOCIAL SCISEARCH. Contains 1,000 abstracted journals of *Social Sciences Citation Index* in various disciplines.

See Also: History; International Affairs.

HEALTH, MEDICINE, AND PSYCHOLOGY

American Psychological Association, *Biographical Directory* (Washington, D.C.: American Psychological Association, 1970 to date). Triennial. Gives brief biographical information on members of affiliated organizations of the association.

Bowker's Medical Books and Serials in Print, 7th ed. (New York: Bowker, 1978). Revised annually. Covers medical literature in all specialties, indexed by subject, author, and title.

Deutsch, Albert (ed.), *The Encyclopedia of Mental Health* (New York: Franklin Watts, 1963), 6 volumes. Meets needs of general readers; includes glossary, bibliography, and detailed index.

English, Horace B., and Champney, Ava, *A Comprehensive Dictionary of Psychological and Psychoanalytical Terms* (New York: David McKay, 1958). Concise definitions.

Harvard University, *The Harvard List of Books in Psychology,* 4th ed. (Cambridge, Mass: Harvard University Press, 1971). Titles indexed by types of psychology.

Index Medicus (Washington: National Library of Medicine, 1960 to date). Monthly. Indexes medical literature since 1879, covering 2,300 journals, indexed by subject and name; with annual cumulations. Also in Medlars Data Base.

Jones, Judith M., *Good Housekeeping Guide to Medicine and Drugs* (New York: Hearst Books, 1977).

Medical Books for the Lay Person, compiled by Marilyn McLean (Boston, Mass: Boston Public Library, 1976). Covers 300 books on diet, health, and medicine.

Merck Manual of Diagnosis and Therapy (Rahway: Merck Sharp & Dohme, 1899 to date). Published for doctors but is easy for general reader to use; arranged by illness and disease; gives information on symptoms, diagnosis, and suggested treatment; has detailed index.

Our Bodies, Ourselves, 2nd ed. (New York: Simon and Schuster, 1976). The bestseller paperback volume for women.

Physicians' Desk Reference (Oradell, N.J.: Medical Economics Company, 1947 to date). Annual volume with information on drug products; available in any library.

Psychological Abstracts (Washington, D.C.: American Psychological Association, 1927 to date). Monthly guide to books and articles, indexed by author and subject; covers 850 reports, journals and documents. Also on Data Base.

Stedman's Medical Dictionary, 23rd ed. (Baltimore: The Williams & Wilkins Co., 1976). Classic work; includes biographical sketches of famous medical persons.

Thompson, William A. R. (ed.), *Black's Medical Dictionary,* 31st ed. (New York: Barnes & Noble, 1977). Standard British directory.

Data Bases

MEDLARS (Medical Literature Retrieval and Analysis System). Stores *Index Medicus.*
PSYCHOLOGICAL ABSTRACTS INFORMATION SERVICES. Stores *Psychological Abstracts.*
CANCERPROJ. Summaries of cancer research worldwide
MEDLARS. Prepared by National Library of Medicine; citations to articles in 3,000 biomedical journals, 1966 to date.

See Also: Libraries of Medical Schools; State and City Departments of Health and Departments of Mental Health; State Medical Directories.

HISTORY

America: History and Life (Santa Barbara, Cal.: American Bibliographical Center-Clio Press, 1964 to date). Three-part guide to over 650 periodicals and journals; abstracts and citations; index to book reviews and listing of dissertations. Also on Data Base.
Atlas of American History, rev. ed. (New York: Scribner's, 1978). Maps show wars, population changes, political, social, and economic conditions in America's history.
Cambridge Ancient History, third ed. (Cambridge, England: University Press, 1923-1939), 12 volumes, 1970; *Cambridge Medieval History,* 2nd ed. (Cambridge, England: University Press, 1911-1936), 8 volumes, 1966; and *New Cambridge Modern History* (Cambridge: University Press, 1957-1970), 13

volumes and atlas. These are the three major reference books in history, available at most medium-size or larger libraries. Well-written articles in all three.

Commager, Henry Steele, *Documents of American History*, 9th ed. (New York: Appleton, 1973), 2 volumes. Useful, chronologically arranged texts of speeches, court cases, treaties, and other documents.

Finley, M. I. (ed.), *Atlas of Classical Archaeology* (New York: McGraw-Hill, 1977). Diagrams, maps and photographs showing classical sites from 1,000 B.C. through A.D. 500.

Freeman-Grenville, G. S. P., *Chronology of World History: A Calendar of Principal Events From 3,000 B.C. to A.D. 1976,* (Totowa, N.J.: Rowman and Littlefield, 1978). Major events, one year at a time; good index.

Freidel, Frank (ed.), *Harvard Guide to American History*, rev. ed. (Cambridge, Mass.: Harvard University Press, 1974), 2 volumes. Good reference for the general reader as well as the scholar; covers all phases and periods; by topical entries; includes reading lists, chronology, subject and name index.

Hammond, H. G. L., and Scullard, H. H. (eds.), *Oxford Classical Dictionary*, 2nd ed. (Oxford, England: Clarendon Press, 1970). Excellent, one-volume work; index to names; includes short bibliographies.

Historical Abstracts (Santa Barbara, Cal.: American Bibliographical Center–Clio Press, 1955 to date). Abstracts articles on world history, excepting U.S. and Canada; quarterly with annual cumulative index.

James, Edward T. (ed.), *Notable American Women, 1607–1950: A Biographical Dictionary,* (Cambridge, Mass.: Harvard University Press, 1971), 3 volumes. Contains 1,359 biographies; the only one of its kind.

Linton, Calvin D. (ed.), *The American Almanac* (New York and Nashville: Thomas Nelson, 1977). Popular paperback, gives major events in America one year at a time.

Morris, R. B., and Morris, Jeffrey B. (eds.), *The Encyclopedia of American History*, bicentennial edition (New York: Harper, 1976). Excellent one-volume work; chronological outlines and topic index; with biographical information also.

Oral History Association, *Oral History in the United States: A Directory*, compiled by Gary L. Shumway (New York: Oral History Research Office of Columbia University, 1971). Describes oral history collections at over 200 institutions.

Times Atlas of World History, The (Maplewood, N.J.: Hammond, Inc., and the London Times, 1978). Good for student and general reader; includes maps, glossary, and indexes.

U.S. Bureau of the Census, *Historical Statistics of the United States: Colonial Times to 1970* (Washington, D.C.: Government Printing Office, 1975), 2 volumes. Tables, statistics, annotations, and sources for further reading on the economic, social, and cultural conditions in America through history. Is usually available at even small libraries and may be purchased at a U.S. Government Bookstore.

Who Was Who in America, Historical Volume, 1607–1896 (Chicago: Marquis Who's Who, Inc., 1967). Covers 13,000 persons, plus events, states, major cities.

Data Bases

AMERICA: HISTORY AND LIFE. See entry above.

See Also: Government, Law; International Affairs; Libraries of graduate schools of history, and historical societies; historical museums.

American Genealogical Research Institute Staff, *How to Trace Your Family Tree: A Complete and Easy to Understand Guide for the Beginner* (Garden City, N.Y.: Doubleday, 1975). Inexpensive paperback.

Buckley, J. C., *The Retirement Handbook,* 6th ed. Revised by H. Schmidt (New York, Harper & Row, 1977). Information on health, income planning, housing, social security, and other related topics; each chapter accompanied by bibliography.

College Blue Book, The, 16th ed. (New York: Macmillan Information, 1977), 5 volumes. Curricula, costs, admissions requirements and other material.

Consumer Reports Annual Buying Guide (Consumer Union of the United States, Inc, 1936 to date). Ratings and evaluations of products.

Fodor, Eugene (ed.), *Fodor's Modern Guides* (New York: McKay, 1953 to date). Popular annual travel guide series covering Europe, Asia, South America, and Japan.

Handbook of Private Schools, The (Boston: Porter Sargent, 1915 to date). Annual. Available in even small libraries; describes 2,000 schools, listed by geographic area.

Hillman, Howard, *The Book of World Cuisines* (New York: Penguin, 1980). Thorough; paperback.

Menke, Frank G., *The Encyclopedia of Sports,* 5th rev. ed. (New York: Barnes & Noble, 1975). Useful for reference to rules, records, history and active organizations in almost all sports, individual and team.

Mobil Travel Guides (Chicago: Rand McNally, 1958 to date). Annual volumes, by region of U.S., evaluating hotels, motels, restaurants, and sites of interest.

Myers, Robert J., *Celebrations: The Complete Book of American Holidays* (Garden City, N.Y.: Doubleday, 1972). Includes a bibliography of sources and illustrations.

National Directory of Addresses and Telephone Numbers, The
(New York: Bantam, 1979). Indispensable listing
of 50,000 numbers to hospitals, businesses, hotels,
airlines, museums, and a myriad of other places in
major U.S. cities. Easy to use.

Post, Elizabeth L., *The New Emily Post's Etiquette* (New York:
Funk & Wagnalls, 1975). Revision of the classic.

Rand McNally Road Atlas (Chicago: Rand McNally). Annual.
Long-time popular map-guide of U.S., Canada, and
Mexico.

Reference Guide for Consumers (New York: Bowker, 1975).
Guide to materials and places for consumer information.

Schuler, Stanley, *How to Fix Almost Everything* (Garden City,
N.Y.: Doubleday, 1966). One of a number of fix-
it guides for household operation.

Taylor, Norman, (ed.), *Taylor's Encyclopedia of Gardening*, 4th
ed. (Boston: Houghton, Mifflin, 1961). Standard
work for amateurs and professionals.

U.S. Department of Agriculture, *Composition of Foods,* Handbook No. 8 (Washington: Government Printing
Office, 1980). Write for a copy.

The World Almanac and Book of Facts (New York: Newspaper
Enterprise Association, 1868 to date). Good, reliable, annual work.

INTERNATIONAL AFFAIRS

Note: *See Also* Chapter Seven.

Britain: An Official Handbook (London: Her Majesty's Sta-
tionery Office). Annual. Guide to economics and
politics.

Countries of the World and Their Leaders, 3rd ed. (Detroit:

Gale, 1976). U.S. State Department's report on nations, including members of governments, political parties, political, economic, and cultural background.

Dickie, John, and Rake, Alan (eds.), *Who's Who in Africa* (London: African Buyer and Trader, Ltd., 1973). Biographies and basic facts for each of 47 countries.

Far East and Australasia, The, 9th ed. (London: Europa Publications, 1977). Government, politics, economic, social, and cultural matters, arranged by region, then subdivisions.

Foreign Affairs Bibliography, 1919 to Date, published for Council on Foreign Relations (New York: Bowker, 1933 to date), 5 volumes. Annotated list of books, each volume covering a ten-year period, up through 1972.

International Who's Who (London: Europa Publications, 1935 to date). A volume of 15,000 brief biographies of world personalities.

South American Handbook (London: Trade and Travel Publications, 1924 to date). Annual directory, country-by-country, includes information about cultural traits, sites to see, etc.

Who's Who in the United Nations and Related Agencies (New York: Arno Press, 1975).

Who's Who in the World, 3rd ed. (Chicago: Marquis Who's Who, Inc., 1977). Lists 25,000 names from 150 countries. *See also* separate Who's Who volumes for individual countries.

Wint, Guy (ed.), *Asia: A Handbook* (New York: Praeger, 1966). Dated but still useful information on the politics, economics, and cultural conditions in Asian countries.

Winton, Harry N. M., *Publications of the United Nations System: A Reference Guide* (New York: Bowker, 1972). Large, annotated list.

LABORDOC. The International Labour Organisation's major publications (books, periodicals, reports, and technical documents) indexed from 1965 to present.

LITERATURE

Bartlett, John (ed.), *Familiar Quotations,* 14th ed. revised and enlarged by E. M. Beck (Boston: Little, Brown, 1968). An old standby, available in paperback; useful key-word index.

Buchanan-Brown, J. (ed.), *Cassell's Encyclopedia of World Literature* (New York: Morrow, 1973) 3 volumes. Another classic, available in even smaller libraries; one volume covers history of literature in countries throughout the world; the other two volumes are biographical.

Cambridge History of English Literature, The (Cambridge, England: University Press, 1907–1927), 15 volumes. One of the classics in the field, this reference history is more an encyclopedia than anything else; available in most libraries of medium-size or larger. Valuable bibliographies. An affordable alternative (about $10 for the paper edition) is *The Concise Cambridge History of English Literature,* 3rd ed., edited by George Sampson, (London: Cambridge University Press, 1970), which includes recent evaluations of Indian, Canadian, Australian, and South African literature as well as the American-English connection.

Contemporary Authors (Detroit: Gale, 1962 to date). Now running up through Volume 72, this work features all writers (excluding those published by "vanity" presses) and is handy when looking for data on little-known authors. The entries are long, much of them written by the authors themselves. Covers 46,000 writers.

Cuddon, J. A. (ed.), *A Dictionary of Literary Terms* (Garden City, N.Y.: Doubleday, 1977). Defines terms, identifies literary forms, styles, and genres; gives bibliographical references.

Essay and General Literature Index (New York: Wilson, 1934 to date). Semiannual. Index to collections of essays, by author and subject; covers only twentieth century writers but includes those from all countries.

Freeman, William, *Dictionary of Fictional Characters,* revised by Fred Urquhart (Boston: The Writer, Inc., 1974). Identifies over 20,000 characters, citing title, author, and date of the work.

Granger's Index to Poetry, 6th ed. (New York: Columbia, 1973). The best way to locate poetry published up through 1970, by either title, first line, author, or subject. References are to 514 anthologies. After 1970, see *Granger's Index to Poetry, 1970–1977;* 119 major anthologies.

Herzberg, Max J., et al., *Reader's Encyclopedia to American Literature* (New York: Crowell, 1962). A complete, useful work, covering every aspect of the literature of America and Canada from the eighteenth century onward — authors, characters, settings, editors, styles and genres; includes biographical and bibliographical information.

Magill, Frank N. (ed.), *Masterplots,* rev. ed. (Englewood Cliffs, N.J.: Salem Press, 1976), 12 volumes. Found in most libraries. Tells plots of over 2,000 works, arranged alphabetically by title.

McGraw-Hill Encyclopedia of World Drama (New York: McGraw-Hill, 1972), 4 volumes. Treats the work of over 1,000 dramatists; summarizes plays, lists works and critical studies, gives biographical and bibliographical information worldwide.

Modern Humanities Research Association, *Annual Bibliography of English Language and Literature, 1920–date,* (Cambridge, England: University Press, 1935 to date). Essential for any student of literature; includes books, magazines, pamphlets.

Ottemiller, John H., *Ottemiller's Index to Plays in Collections,* edited by John M. and Billie M. Connor, 6th ed., revised and enlarged (Metuchen, N.J.: Scarecrow, 1976).

Play Index, 1953–1978 (New York: Wilson, 1949 to 1977), 5 volumes. Includes all kinds of plays in collections: radio, tv, Broadway plays, plays for children; indexed by author, title, and subject; summarizes plots, gives casts, sets, and other data.

Rush, Theressa, and Myers, Carol F., *Black American Writers Past and Present: A Biographical and Bibliographical Dictionary* (Metuchen, N.J.: Scarecrow, 1975), 2 volumes. Covers 2,000 writers from eighteenth century through 1973; includes bibliography.

Selective Bibliography for the Study of English and American Literature, 5th ed. (New York: Macmillan, 1975). One of the best guides to what is available in the reference field. Good for nonspecialist as well as scholar.

Short Story Index, and *Supplements* (New York: Wilson, 1953–1974), 6 volumes. Annual supplements for 1974 to date. If you know the author or title of a story, this work will tell you where to find it.

Sutton, Robert B., *Speech Index,* 4th ed., revised and enlarged, (New York: Scarecrow, 1966). Covers speeches in more than 250 collections published through 1965. Two *Supplements* cover 1966–1975.

Watson, George (ed.), *The New Cambridge Bibliography of English Literature* (Cambridge, England: University

Press, 1969-1977), 5 volumes. Works by and about authors in primary and secondary source materials.

PERFORMING ARTS
(INCLUDING FILM AND TELEVISION)

American Film Institute, *The American Film Institute Catalog of Motion Pictures Produced in the United States* (New York: Bowker, 1971). Still in the works, this valuable work covers feature films (1911-1970); shorts (1911-1970) and newsreels (1908-1970) giving full particulars — casts, production crews, plot summaries, etc.

Baker, Theodore, *Biographical Dictionary of Musicians,* 5th ed., revised by Nicolas Slonimsky, with 1971 supplement (New York: G. Schirmer). The best standard work in the field; a few popular musicians covered but mostly older composers, singers, pianists, arrangers, etc. 16,000 entries with bibliographies.

Best Plays Of . . . , The (New York: Dodd, 1899 to date). Even small, country libraries tend to have this series. A new volume appears at the end of each "season", giving abridged texts of the 10 best plays plus other information (statistics, awards, records). Index volume to most of the series is *Directory of the American Theater, 1894-1971,* also published by Dodd.

Blum, Eleanor, *Basic Books in the Mass Media* (Urbana, Ill.: University of Illinois, 1972). Indexes books, periodicals, and other material.

Broadcasting Yearbook (Washington, D.C.: Broadcasting Publications). Annual. The must-have volume for anyone in the business.

Brown, Les, *The New York Times Encyclopedia of Television* (New York: Quadrangle/The New York Times,

1977). Historical and other information on personalities, shows, networks, cable and pay-T.V., rules, and regulations.

Dance Encyclopedia, The, compiled by Anatole Chujoy and P. W. Manchester, revised and enlarged edition (New York: Simon & Schuster, 1967). Standard work covering the entire field.

Guide to Corporate Giving in the Arts, A, compiled and edited by Susan E. Wagner (New York: American Council for the Arts, 1978). You can't afford not to buy this (sells for under $13) if you have anything to do with raising money for the arts. Tells who gave how much to whom and for what.

Hartnoll, Phyllis (ed.), *The Oxford Companion to the Theatre,* (New York: Oxford, 1967). Defines terms, gives information on actors, theatres, producers, dramatists.

International Motion Picture Almanac (New York: Quigley Publications Company, 1929 to date). Annual. Required if you're in the industry (or want to be); fun if you're not. Includes who's who and other lists of sources.

International Television Almanac (New York: Quigley Publications Company, 1956 to date). Younger sibling of the above.

Kobbé, Gustave, *The New Kobbé's Complete Opera Book,* edited and revised by the Earl of Harewood (New York: Putnam, 1976). The standard guide to opera, covers 300 operas of past 300 years; information on performances, plot, score, libretto, etc.

Koegler, Horst, *The Concise Oxford Dictionary of Ballet* (New York: Oxford University Press, 1977). Four hundred years of ballet: sources, summaries, terms, dancers, choreographers, schools, theaters, and a little bit on ethnic, ballroom, and modern dance.

Music Index: The Key to Current Music Periodical Literature (Detroit: Information Coordinators, 1949 to date).

Monthly reference to biographies as well as over 300 periodicals; indexed by author and subject; annual cumulations.

New Grove Dictionary of Music and Musicians, The (New York: Macmillan, 1978), 14 volumes (an edition is available in paper). *The* encyclopedia in music; 12,000 articles on composers; lists works, bibliographies and sources for information; alphabetical arrangement with cross-references. If your library doesn't have this, stick with the *International Cyclopedia of Music and Musicians* (see page 226).

New York Times Film Reviews, 1913–1968, The (New York: New York Times and Arno, 1970), 6 volumes. Chronological arrangement of 17,000 reviews with indexes to titles, persons, and corporations.

New York Times Theater Reviews, 1920–1974, The (New York: New York Times and Arno, 1971–1975), 10 volumes. Index, 2 volumes. Indexed by personal names and production companies as well as titles.

Pavlakis, Christopher, *The American Music Handbook* (New York: Free Press, 1974). As much about the music business as it is about the subject of music; includes data on budgets, recordings, band and opera companies, festivals and camps, publishers, etc., with detailed index.

Popular Music Periodicals Index (Metuchen, N.J.: Scarecrow, 1974 to date) Annual, valuable supplement to *Music Index,* covers 50 periodicals.

Scheuer, Steven H. (ed.), *Movies on TV, 1978–79 Edition* (New York: Bantam Books, 1977). New editions to come, an alphabetical listing of over 10,000 films, rated by the star-system. Inexpensive paperback gives plot, cast and production information and a good idea of whether a movie is worth putting up with the commercials.

Sharp, Harold S., and Sharp, M. Z., *Index to Characters in the*

Performing Arts (Methuchen, N.J.: Scarecrow, 1966-1973) 6 volumes. Guide indexing 73,000 major and minor characters in plays, ballets, operas, television shows, etc.

Stambler, Irwin, *Encyclopedia of Pop, Rock, and Soul* (New York: St. Martin's, 1974). A good source but how do you keep it up to date? The only answer is an almanac, which is bound to come out soon. Also, does not include country and western.

Thompson, Oscar, *The International Cyclopedia of Music and Musicians,* 10th ed. edited by Bruce Bohle (New York: Dodd, 1975). Most useful one-volume work on all aspects of music — notation, styles, criticism, schools, and more.

Who's Who in the Theatre: A Biographical Record of the Contemporary Stage, 16th ed. (Detroit: Gale, 1976). Entries on actors, producers, directors, dramatists, designers; lists productions; long runs; playbills; from 1870 on; Broadway, off-Broadway; London.

See Also: Schools of Drama and Music; special performing arts libraries or museums; film archives; film rental companies (free or inexpensive catalogs are available, giving detailed information on movies); music, drama, dance, film, and television associations.

PHILOSOPHY AND RELIGION

Adams, Charles J. (ed.), *A Reader's Guide to the Great Religions,* 2nd ed. (New York: The Free Press, 1977). Bibliographic essays; includes ancient and primitive religions as well.

AlFarqui, Isma'il, and Sopher, David, (eds.), *Historical Atlas of the Religions of the World,* (New York: Macmillan, 1974). Maps, bibliographies, and chronologies covering all religions, past and present.

American Theological Library Association, *Index to Religious Periodical Literature*, 1949/1954 to date (Chicago: American Theological Library Association, 1953 to date). Annual until 1962, biennial thereafter. Indexes more than 150 periodicals by author and subject.

Barrow, John G., *A Bibliography of Bibliographies in Religion* (Ann Arbor, Mich.: Edwards, 1955). Thorough index to authors, titles, and subjects.

Directory of American Scholars, 6th ed. (New York: Bowker, 1974) Volume IV, Philosophy, Religion, and Law.

Encyclopaedia Judaica (New York: Macmillan, 1972), 16 volumes. Includes bibliographies, biographical articles and a wealth of information. Supplemented by a *Yearbook*, 1973 to date.

Encyclopedia of Philosophy (New York: Macmillan, 1973), 4 volumes. Available in most libraries; contains 1,450 articles by over 500 contributors; alphabetically arranged; with annotated bibliography; for the nonspecialist.

Gibb, H. A. R., et al., *Encyclopedia of Islam*, new edition (Leiden, Netherlands: Brill, 1954). Note date; yet a thorough treatment of Islamic culture, history, and religion.

Hastings, James, *Dictionary of the Bible*, rev. ed. by Frederick C. Grant and H. H. Rowley (New York: Scribner's, 1963).

International Directory of Philosophy and Philosophers, 1st ed. (Bowling Green, Ohio: Philosophy Documentation Center, 1966 to date). Biennial guide to the entire field; includes societies, schools, research centers, etc. Companion volume is *Directory of American Philosophers*, 1962 to date, from the same publisher, which gives information on college and university faculty in the field.

Lacey, A. R., *A Dictionary of Philosophy* (Boston: Routledge & Kegan Paul, Ltd., 1976). Good for students;

some biographies; some bibliographies; also available in paperback (Scribner's).

Mead, Frank Spencer, *Handbook of Denominations in the United States,* 5th ed. (Nashville, Tenn.: Abingdon Press, 1970). Statistical data, glossary, history, doctrines, and structure of over 250 religious bodies; includes bibliography.

Nelson's Complete Concordance of the Revised Standard Version of the Bible, compiled under the supervision of John W. Ellison (New York: Thomas Nelson & Sons, 1957). A concordance gives the context and location of each key word; there are many concordances to the varying versions of the Bible, several of which will be available even in small libraries.

New Catholic Encyclopedia, The, prepared by an editorial staff at the Catholic University of America, (New York: McGraw-Hill, 1967), 15 volumes. Everything, from beginning to present time. There is also a *Supplement, 1967–1974,* edited by David Eggenberger, from the same publisher.

Parrinder, Geoffrey, *A Dictionary of Non-Christian Religions,* (Philadelphia: Westminster Press, 1971). Defines terms, doctrines, etc. for ancient and contemporary religions.

Philosopher's Index: An International Index to Philosophical Periodicals, The (Bowling Green, Ohio: Bowling Green University, 1967 to date). Covers over 80 journals, quarterly; indexed by key-word for subject and author.

See Also: Denomination handbooks (*American Jewish Yearbook; Official Catholic Directory;* each one has its own); graduate schools of philosophy and divinity or theology school libraries.

Note: Obviously, the nature of your business or field will require that you consult the basic works listed in other categories in this Appendix. Yet there are several general works that might be of use.

Haines, Virginia and Ryan, Catherine, (eds.) *Dictionary for Secretaries* (Los Angeles, Cal.: Parker & Sons, 1971).

Hotel and Motel Red Book (New York: American Hotel and Motel Association Directory Corp., 1886 to date). Annual. Arranged by city and state, contains basic information on facilities, including prices; no rating system.

Hutchinson, Lois Irene, *Standard Handbook for Secretaries,* 8th ed. (New York: McGraw-Hill, 1977). Modern and doesn't "talk down" to the reader; covers grammar, spelling, letter writing; meetings; and report writing.

National Directory of Addresses and Telephone Numbers, 1980–81 (New York: Bantam, 1979). Buy it; it has every number you'll ever need on the job that isn't in your boss's own telephone file.

Post, Elizabeth L., *The New Emily Post's Etiquette* (New York: Funk & Wagnalls, 1975).

Webster's Secretarial Handbook (Springfield, Mass.: G. & C. Merriam Co., 1976) A much-used work; alternative to the Hutchinson title above.

World Almanac and Book of Facts, The (New York: Newspaper Enterprise Association, 1868 to date) It's under $3, so splurge and buy the new one each year; have either this or another almanac on your desk.

Note: There are so many branches of the sciences and so many subspecialties within those branches that it would be foolish for a layperson to even attempt a basic books list. What follows, then, are merely a few of the more general reference works (indexes, biographies, bibliographies, etc.) that are available in most libraries and can be used by the general reader. At least you'll have a starting point for a search in the sciences.

American Men and Women of Science, 13th ed. (New York: Bowker, 1976), 7 volumes. Current biographies on American and Canadian scientists; the volumes cover the various branches within the sciences.

Applied Science & Technology Index (New York: Wilson, 1958 to date). Monthly except July, with periodic cumulations. A subject index to 200 journals in the sciences, from aeronautics to metallurgy; good for the general reader having to search for information within a branch.

Collocott, T. C. (ed.), *Dictionary of Science and Technology* (London: W & R. Chambers, Ltd., 1971). Definitions.

Dictionary of Scientific Biography, published under the auspices of the American Council of Learned Societies (New York: Scribner's, 1970–76), 14 volumes. Volume 15, *Supplement,* 1977; Volume 16, *Index,* 1978. Lives of 5,000 scientists from all periods, all deceased; each biography contains a bibliography.

General Science Index (New York: Wilson, 1978 to date). Monthly, except June and December, with annual cumulation. Subject index to 88 general science periodicals.

Industrial Research Laboratories of the United States, 15th ed. (New York: Bowker, 1977). Who's doing research for whom and on what.

Klein, Barry (ed.), *Guide to American Scientific and Technical Directories*, 2nd ed., (Rye, New York: Todd Publications, 1975). Guide to over 2500 directories in the sciences.

Lasworth, Earl, *Reference Sources in Science and Technology* (Metuchen, N.J.: Scarecrow, 1972).

McGraw-Hill Dictionary of Scientific and Technical Terms, 2nd ed. (New York: McGraw-Hill, 1978). The best when you're starting from scratch — 100,000 definitions with diagrams, charts, photographs, and drawings.

McGraw-Hill Encyclopedia of Science and Technology, 4th ed. (New York: McGraw-Hill, 1977), 15 volumes. The best science encyclopedia, used by novices and experts. There are annual *Yearbooks* as well.

Malinowsky, Harold R., *Science and Engineering Literature: A Guide to Reference Sources*, 2nd ed., (Littleton, Col.: Libraries Unlimited, 1976). Gives advice on how to make a search in the sciences; annotated list of sources.

National Technical Information Service, United States Department of Commerce, *Current Published Searches from the NTIS Bibliographic Data File* (NTIS, Fall, 1979). You obtain this through the mail from NTIS, but it's worth waiting for; gives list of already published searches (with over 200 abstracts per average search) of over 680,000 reports summarizing government or government-funded research projects; the catalog has an easy-to-use subject index (there is a title index as well) ranging from "Ablation" to "X-rays." When you've located a specific report that fits your needs, you then buy it from NTIS.

Science and Technology Division, National Referral Center, *A Directory of Information Resources in the United States*, rev. ed. (Washington, D.C.: Library of

Congress, 1974). A valuable guide, arranged alphabetically, by agency or commission, with a subject index in the back.

Scientific, Technical, and Related Societies of the United States, 9th ed. (Washington, D.C.: National Academy of Sciences, 1971). Lists names, addresses, history, membership requirements, activities, publications of them all.

Data Bases

COMPENDEX. *Engineering Index Monthly* is stored here, from 1970 on; engineering and math.

ENVIROLINE. Periodicals, government reports, documents, industry studies, articles, films and monographs in the realm of environmental literature, 1971 to date.

NTIS. Provides 550,000 citations to unrestricted government sponsored research reports in the sciences, 1970 to date. Available on the three major data base systems.

PATENTS. Largest patents data base; stores patent information on 10,000 patents issued weekly by 20 leading industrial nations.

POPINFORM. Articles, reports, etc. on the subject of fertility control, 1972 to date.

SCISEARCH. The major storage base of citations to most of the world's scientific journals, 1974 to date.

See Also: Health, Medicine, and Psychology in this appendix.

FOR WRITERS, RESEARCHERS, AND EDITORS

Note: The freelance writer or researcher is often the generalist of generalists and therefore may have to consult at least one book in each of the categories in this appendix at one time or another. This category singles out works about getting information, along with other reference tools the writer needs in order to live. In fact, the books and numbers cited in Chapter Two, though they may be of interest to others, are "must haves" for anyone engaged in full-time writing or research.

The Alumni (Alumnae) Directory of your college or university; and any Career Counseling Directory that may be issued by your alma mater. You never can tell when a former classmate may provide you with the link you need in a search for information.

American Society for Information Science, *Computer-Readable Data Bases* (Urbana, Ill.: ASIS, University of Illinois, 1979). An excellent, detailed source of information on 528 data bases.

Bell, Marion V., and Swidan, Eleanor A., *Reference Books: A Brief Guide*, 8th ed. (Baltimore: Enoch Pratt Free Library, 1978). Costs $2.50, from the Library, and well worth it. Fits in your pocket so you can take it to the library with you to direct you in your search beginnings. Discusses types of reference materials, then specific sources, arranged by subjects.

Brady, John, *The Craft of Interviewing* (New York: Random House, Vintage Books, 1977). A chatty paperback on getting interviews, doing background for them, and then conducting them. Very anecdotal, but some sound suggestions.

Burack, A. S. (ed.), *Writer's Handbook* (Boston: The Writer, Inc., 1977). Annual guide on freelance writing and markets for your work.

Carroll, John M., *Confidential Information Sources: Public & Private* (Los Angeles: Security World Books, 1975). Who uses what kind of information, how he or she gets it, and to what uses it is put.

Contact Book (New York: Celebrity Service, Inc., 1980). Annual directory of "contacts" in the world of film, stage, publishing, sports, television, restaurants, etc. in Hollywood, New York, Paris, London, and Rome. A tempting buy to any writer at only $8.00.

Cottam, Keith M., and Pelton, Robert W., *Writer's Research Handbook* (New York: A. S. Barnes & Co., 1977). List of reference sources and some tips.

Editor & Publisher International Year Book (New York: Editor & Publisher). Annual. The directory of the newspaper industry.

Gates, Jean Key, *Guide to the Use of Books and Libraries*, 4th ed. (New York: McGraw-Hill, 1979). Not as thorough as Katz's book (see entry below) and perhaps not as handy as the Bell and Swidan book (see entry above); but good, anyway.

Herman, Lewis, *A Practical Manual of Screen Playwriting for Theater and Television Films* (New York: New American Library, 1952). In paper; a how-to that covers all aspects of the craft, from story idea to filmic components.

How to Publish, Promote & Sell Your Book, rev. ed. (Chicago: Adams Press, 1977).

Hudson's Washington News Media Contacts Directory (Washington, D.C.: Hudson). Annual. Lists correspondents, editors, columnists, commentators, and freelance writers in Washington.

International Directory of Little Magazines and Small Presses (Paradise, Cal.: Dustbooks). Annual. Outlets for your work; names of editors; requirements; payment; etc.

Katz, William A., *Introduction to Reference Work, Volume I: Basic Information Sources* (New York: McGraw-Hill, 1978). It's supposedly written for librarians, but can certainly be used and understood by anyone. It's the best — a critical, annotated discussion (as opposed to merely a list) of most reference works.

Literary Market Place, 1979–1980 (New York: Bowker, 1979).

The must-have directory in the field of publishing; valuable for the writer; lists publishers, columnists, agents; prizes; fellowships; clubs and societies and sources for information.

O'Neill, Carol L., and Ruder, Avima, *The Complete Guide to Editorial Freelancing* (New York: Dodd, Mead & Co., 1974). Editing, copyediting, proofreading, indexing, and other skills; how to do them and for whom.

Sanders, James B., Consultant editor, *Information Market Place, 1978-79,* (New York: Bowker, 1978). Lists 5,000 companies or individuals who deal in information products and services; includes data bases and indexes.

Sheehy, Eugene P., *Guide to Reference Books,* 9th ed. (Chicago: American Library Association, 1976). Another good one, favored by many librarians.

Strunk, William J., and White, E. B., *The Elements of Style,* 2nd ed. (New York: Macmillan, 1972). The most popular guidebook on how to write in English.

Wallechinsky, David, and Wallace, Irving, *The Book of Lists* (New York: Morrow, 1977) The bestseller. Many writers find it helpful for (1) giving them ideas; and (2) escaping writing.

1980 Writer's Market (Cincinnati, Ohio: Writers's Digest Books, 1979). Where to sell what you write. Important.

Wynar, Bohdan S. (ed.), *Reference Books in Paperback* (Littleton, Col.: Libraries Unlimited, 1976). Arranged by subject; a selected, annotated listing of 675 books.

SOURCES FOR PICTURES

A.L.A. Portrait Index (Washington, D.C.: Government Printing Office, 1906). For finding portraits of persons living up through the nineteenth century; covers 40,000 persons, portraits in many publications.

Bartran, Margaret, *A Guide to Color Reproductions,* 2nd ed. (Metuchen, N.J.: Scarecrow, 1971). Lists over 12,000 color reproductions you can buy from various publishers. Arranged by artist; has title index as well.

Cirker, Hayward, and Cirker, Blanche (eds.), *Dictionary of American Portraits* (New York: Dover, 1967). Over 4,000 portraits (drawings, engravings, photos, etc.) of famous men and women.

Ellis, Jessie C., *Index to Illustrations* (Boston: Faxon, 1967). Covers all fields, mostly illustrations appearing in books.

Evans, Hilary; Evans, Mary; and Nelki, Andra, *The Picture Researcher's Handbook: An International Guide to Picture Sources and How to Use Them* (New York: Scribner's, 1974). Part One is general information and terminology; Part Two is a country-by-country listing of collections with information on services, specialties, hours, fees, etc.; Part Three contains indexes — geographic, by specialized subject, and alphabetical source.

Literary Market Place, 1979–1980 (New York: Bowker, 1980). A section on "Photo & Picture Sources" describes various collections in archives, stock agencies, etc.

1980 Writer's Market (Cincinnati, Ohio: Writer's Digest Books, 1979). See its chapter, "Picture Sources."

SOURCES — WHERE TO FIND PROFESSIONAL RESEARCHERS

American Society of Journalists and Authors, 123 W. 43rd Street, New York, N.Y. 10036. The ASJA's *Membership Directory* costs $25 and includes writers and their subject specialties, listed by geographic area. Or, you can "Dial A Writer" at the ASJA, (212) 586-7136 for a recommendation.

FIND/SVP, The Information Clearinghouse, 500 Fifth Avenue, New York, N.Y. 10036, a full-service research firm describes its functions in *The Booklet of Knowledge For Business People*, a promotional piece obtainable from FIND.

Information Industry Association, *Information Sources, 1978-79 Membership Directory*, describes the services offered by over 100 companies. May also be available in your library or can be obtained from the Association in Bethesda, Maryland, for about $10.

Information Market Place, 1978-79, A Directory of Information Products and Services, Consultant editor, James B. Sanders, (New York: Bowker, 1978) Includes 5,000 firms and individuals in the information business.

"Information Services for Business, Industry, Government From the Georgia Tech Library," Information Exchange Center, Price Gilbert Memorial Library, Georgia Institute of Technology, Atlanta, Georgia 30332. A pamphlet describing their research services, which include searching (computer and manual), verifying citations, interlibrary loans, translations, reproduction and location of material not in libraries; includes a schedule of fees for each service. This is a pretty good sample of the research services provided by some university libraries. It is always worth checking a school library or school of library science near where you work or live to see if such a service exists.

Kruzas, Anthony T. (ed.), *Encyclopedia of Information Systems & Services*, 3rd ed. (Detroit: Gale, 1978). Describes 1,750 organizations in the information business.

Literary Market Place, 1979–1980 (New York: Bowker, 1980). See "For Writers" in this appendix.

Other representative university libraries that offer freelance research services include: Regional Information and Communication Exchange, "Ask A Question!" Rice University Library, P.O. Box 1892, Houston, Texas 77001; and the School of Information Studies, Continuing Education Program at Syracuse University, Syracuse, New York. Ask for their "Directory of Free-Lance Librarians and Information Brokers."

Translator Referral Directory, 1977, 3rd ed., Guild of Professional Translators, 5914 Pulaski Avenue, Philadelphia, Pa. 19144. Listing of 125 registered professional translators, representing 46 languages, with names, numbers, and subject specialties; available for $4 from the Guild.

Warner-Eddison Associates is another professional research business, this one in Lexington, Massachusetts (55 Waltham Street, P.O. Box 254). They issue descriptive promotional material.

Washington Independent Writers Association, The (at the National Press Building, Suite 13, Terrace Level, Washington, D.C. 20045) will find the right researcher for your needs in the Washington area, including extensive searching among government material.

Washington Researchers (918 Sixteenth Street, N.W., Washington, D.C. 20006) is another large research firm that works mostly for business. "Washington Researchers" is a fat folder of material describing the firm's services, publications, and conferences.

Washington Service Bureau (1225 Connecticut Avenue, N.W., Washington, D.C. 20036) is another large, much-used-by-business firm. "Government Information Is Our Business" is its portfolio of services and publications.

Wasserman, Paul, and McLean, Janice (eds.), *Consultants and Consulting Organizations Directory*, 3rd ed. (Detroit: Gale, 1976).

1980 Writer's Market (Cincinnati, Ohio: Writer's Digest Books, 1979). See its section on "Writers' Organizations" for additional ideas on where to go for help.

INDEX

240